東南亞史研究 7

真臘風土記中英文對照本
Record on the Custom and Land of Zhen-la
(Chinese v. English Version)

作者：周達觀

Author: Zhou Da-guan

譯者：陳鴻瑜

Translator: Chen Hurng Yu

（附白話文翻譯）

(with vernacular translation)

蘭臺出版社

譯者序

Translator's Preface

　　元朝人周達觀寫的書，直至一百多年後明朝才見世出版，以後也沒有引起多大的迴響。中國古籍也幾乎沒有有關吳哥王朝的建築物之記載和報導。這對於愛好文明的中國人而言，是很令人驚訝的事。

　　The book of Zhou Da-guan was written in the Yuan Dynasty, but it was not published until more than one hundred years later in the Ming Dynasty. Thereafter, this book did not arouse much widespread interest. Even those Chinese annals or other books scarcely mention the Angkor Kingdom's architecture. It is a surprising thing for the Chinese who especially love civilization and culture.

　　西方人開始對吳哥城之注意，始於 1819 年法國人雷慕沙（Abel Rémusat）以法文翻譯真臘風土記，書名為中國旅行者在第十三世紀末訪問柬埔寨王國之描述（*Description du royaume de Camboge [sic] par un voyageur chinois qui a visité cette contrée à la fin du XIIIe siècle*）。法國自然學家毛哈特（Henri Mouhot）在 1860 年 2-4 月到吳哥寺進行測量神廟，1864 年出版他的日記筆記，吳哥城才受到西方人的重視。1902 年伯希和（Paul Pelliot）又將該書譯成法文（*Mémoires sur les coutumes du Cambodge de Tcheou Ta-kouan*）。1940 年，

日本外務省調查部譯編真臘風土記為日文。1951 年，根據伯希和遺作整理出版的回顧周達觀的真臘風土記：伯希和遺作新編（*Chen La Feng Tuchi, Mémoires sur les coutumes du Cambodge de Tcheou Ta-kouan / version nouvelle suivie d'un commentaire inachevé [par] Paul Pelliot*）。1967 年，J. Gilman d'Acry Paul 根據伯希和 1902 年譯本翻譯成英文的真臘風土記註解（*Notes on the Customs of Cambodia*）。1971 年柬埔寨人李添丁的真臘風土記柬文版在金邊出版。1989 年，日本人和田久德譯注真臘風土記：吳哥時期的柬埔寨（真臘風土記：アンコール期のカンボジア）。

The Westerners began to pay attention to the Angkor architecture after the Frenchman Abel Rémusat translated Zhou's book as *Description du royaume de Camboge [sic] par un voyageur chinois qui a visité cette contrée à la fin du XIIIe siècle* in 1819. Another French naturalist, Henri Mouhot, went to Angkor to survey temples from February to April 1860, and his diary was published in 1864. After that, the Angkor architecture became popular in Western society. Frenchman Paul Pelliot translated Zhou's book as *Mémoires sur les coutumes du Cambodge de Tcheou Ta-kouan*. The Department of Investigation of the Ministry of Foreign Affairs of Japan translated Zhou's book into a Japanese version in 1940. In 1951, the Paris bookstore Adrien-Maisonneuve published the *Chen La Feng Tuchi, Mémoires sur les coutumes du Cambodge de Tcheou Ta-kouan / version nouvelle suivie d'un commentaire inachevé [par] Paul Pelliot*. In 1967, J. Gilman d'Acry Paul utilized the 1902 version of Paul Pelliot's book to publish the *Notes on the Customs of*

Cambodia. A Cambodian, Ly Thong Teng, translated Zhou's book into a Cambodian version. In 1989, a Japanese Hisada Wada translated and annotated Zhou's book into a Japanese version.

　　第一本真臘風土記英文全譯本,是由 Michael Smithies 於 2001 年出版的柬埔寨風俗習慣 (*The Customs of Cambodia*)。 2006 年,德國人 Guido Keller 翻譯出版德文版周達觀：柬埔寨的風俗習慣,第十三世紀吳哥的生活 (*Chou Ta-Kuan: Sitten in Kambodscha. Über das Leben in Angkor im 13. Jahrhundert*)。 2007 年,紐西蘭人 Peter Harris 翻譯出版英文版真臘風土記 (書名 *A Record of Cambodia: The Land and Its People*)。2010 年,柬埔寨人 Solang Uk 和 Beling Uk 將該書譯成英文。2011 年,越南人何萬丹 (Hà, Văn Tấn)、潘輝黎 (Phan, Huy Lê) 和阮玉福 (Nguyễn, Ngọc Phúc) 將該書翻譯成越文。

The first complete English translation of Zhou's book was *The Customs of Cambodia* which was translated and published by Michael Smithies in 2001. A German, Guido Keller, translated Zhou's book as *Chou Ta-Kuan: Sitten in Kambodscha. Über das Leben in Angkor im 13. Jahrhundert*. Peter Harris, a New Zealander, who can read Chinese, translated Zhou's book into English *A Record of Cambodia: The Land and Its People* in 2007. The Cambodian, Solang Uk, and Beling Uk translated Zhou's book into an English version in 2010. The Vietnamese, Hà, Văn Tấn, Phan, Huy Lê and Nguyễn, Ngọc Phúc, translated Zhou's book into a Vietnamese version in 2011.

　　以上英文翻譯家對於真臘風土記之翻譯,因為係非中文為母語語系的關係,還是有若干詞句翻譯有出入。因此,本人遂興起一股想譯出一本較為符合原意的英文版,俾讓西方讀者對該書內容有正確的理解。

All versions of the above English translations contain some translation mistakes probably due to Chinese not being the mother tongue of the translator. Thus I decided to create a more precise version of Zhou's book in order to help Westerners to understand his book.

陳鴻瑜謹誌
Chen Hurng Yu

2023 年 5 月 4 日
May 4, 2023

目次

Contents

圖目次

Table of figures

譯者之導論

Translator's Introduction

陳鴻瑜撰

By Chen Hurng Yu

一、透過周達觀瞭解元朝與真臘的關係

1. To understand the relationship between the Yuan Dynasty and Zhen-la through Zhou Da-guan

周達觀是元世祖和元成宗統治中國時期的人物，他在1296 年 8 月出使抵達真臘，今之柬埔寨，於 1297 年 6 月返國寫了真臘風土記一書，作為他的返國報告。周達觀在該著作的總敘中提及唆都元帥在攻打占城時，設置了征占城行省，他派遣一虎符萬戶、一金牌千戶到真臘招諭，但遭到拘執而沒有返國。因此，元成宗在 1295 年 6 月再度遣使到真臘招諭，周達觀為其隨從。

Zhou Da-guan was a person when the Yuan Dynasty emperors Shi-zu and Cheng-zung ruled China, arrived at Zhen-la in August 1296. Zhen-la is nowadays Cambodia. Zhou Da-guan returned to China in June 1297 and wrote a book: *Record on the Custom and Land of Zhen-la*. He mentioned in the general preface that Marshall Sordu set up a Conquer-Champa Moving-Province to attack Champa, and sent two generals to inform Zhen-la to send a mission to China, but both officials were captured and didn't return. Therefore the Yuan emperor Cheng-zung sent another mission to Zhen-la in June 1295. Zhou Da-guan was in the retinue of this mission.

據上述記載來檢視元朝和真臘的關係。

According to the above historic record, we could review the relationships between the Yuan Dynasty and Zhen-la.

1280 年，元朝出兵攻打占城，以占城國王孛由補剌者吾稱臣內附，命唆都就其國立占城行省撫之。1281 年 10 月，元朝在占城設立「征占城行中書省」，準備海船百艘，新舊軍及水手合萬人，期以明年正月征海外諸番，除了要求占城給軍糧外，又遣使招諭干不昔（即真臘）來歸附，[1] 但未獲回應。

In 1280, the Yuan Dynasty attacked Champa and repressed King Bor-yo-bu-la-jer-wu who surrendered to the Yuan. The Yuan Dynasty ordered Marshall Sordu to set up a Conquer-Champa Moving-Province to placate the local people.

In October 1281, the Yuan Dynasty set up a Conquer-

---

[1] [明]宋濂等撰，元史，本紀第十一，世祖八，楊家駱主編，新校本元史並附編二種，鼎文書局，台北市，民國 66 年，頁 234-235。

[Ming] Song Lien, et al., *Yuan Shi(A History of Yuan Dynasty)*, Main Record, No.11, Shi Zu, No.8, in Yang Jialuo(ed.), *The New Proofreading of Yuan Shi and Two Attachments*, Ding-wen Bookstore, Taipei, 1977, pp. 234-235.

Champa Moving Zhongshu Province[2] and prepared hundreds of ships, new and old soldiers and sailors numbering over ten thousand, for conquering overseas foreign countries in the following January. Besides asking that Champa provide food and dispatch a mission to inform Gan-bu-shih (namely Zhen-la) to send a mission to China and submit their vassal status to China. But there was not any response from Zhen-la.

1282 年 6 月，占城王子補的（或寫為補底）反抗元朝。10 月，元朝命唆都、唐兀斛等領兵伐占城。10 月，占城國王遣使稱臣內屬，遂命右丞索都等即其地立省，以撫安之。元朝為了攻打補的反抗軍，在 12 月遣使招真臘國使色呼默請往占城招諭，結果得知占城已做了戰爭的準備：「已脩木城，備甲兵，刻期請戰。」[3]因此占城和元朝雙方持續戰爭到 1284 年 11 月，占城才求和入貢。

In June 1282, Bu-de, the prince of Champa, fought against the Yuan Dynasty. In October, Marshall Sordu and Tang Yuan-hu again led the army to attack Champa. In October, the Champa king sent a mission to China and paid tribute. Marshall Sordu set up an Moving-province to placate the people. In order to attack the opposition forces of Bu-de,

---

[2] 中書省是中央政府的機構名稱。

Zhongshu Province is the name of the central government.

[3] [民國]柯邵忞撰，新元史，卷之二百十，列傳第九十七，占城條，成文出版社，台北市，1971 年，頁 8-10。

[Republic of China] Ke Shaomin, *New History of Yuan*, volume 210, biography, No.97, Champa, Chengwen Publishing Company, Taipei, 1971, pp. 8-10.

the Yuan Dynasty sent a mission to Zhen-la to ask their envoy Sir-le-mor to Champa, to persuade Champa to surrender to China. But Sir-le-mor delivered Champa's answer: "Champa had already recovered the capital Mu-Chen (namely Vijaya), prepared its military, and was inviting a war with China." Since then, both China and Champa fought continuingly up to November of 1284. Then, Champa asked for peace and paid the tribute to China.

儘管史書記載真臘和占城在 1285 年 9 月對中國貢樂工十人及藥材、鱷魚皮諸物。[4]但史書沒有記載為何真臘在此時向元朝進貢，一個最大可能是真臘商人載運藥材和鱷魚皮到中國進行貿易，而被寫為進貢。

Despite the historical annals recording Zhen-la and Champa paying tribute to ten musicians, medicinal herbs and crocodile skins, etc., to China in September 1285, that book didn't mention the reason why both countries paid tribute to China at this time. It is probable that there were businessmen who brought goods to China to do business and that was wrongly written down as coming to offer tribute.

1292 年 7 月，元朝出兵遠征爪哇，當時中書右丞阿里願自備船，同張存從征爪哇軍，他們在行抵占城時，被派往占城和甘不察招諭。忽必烈詔授阿里三珠虎符，張存

---

[4] [明]宋濂等撰，元史，本紀第十三，世祖十，頁 279。

[Ming] Song Lien, et al., *Yuan Shi*(*A History of Yuan Dynasty*), Main Record, No.13, Shi Zu, No.10, in Yang Jialuo(ed.), *op.cit.*, p.279.

一珠虎符。[5]甘不察就是柬埔寨之不同音譯。周達觀書中所講的兩使者到真臘沒有回國者，應是阿里和張存。周達觀的書說他們兩位是由征占城行省所派，其實是由征爪哇遠征軍到達占城時所派。

In July 1292, the Yuan dispatched military forces to attack Java. Right Prime Minister Ali voluntarily prepared himself ships to carry out an assault on Java with Chang Tshun. When the expedition army arrived at Champa, Ali, and Chang Tshun were sent to Champa and Gan-bu-tcha to demand both countries send their mission to China. Yuan Emperor Kublai Khan granted Ali a three-jewel Tiger Talisman[6] and Chang Tshun a one-jewel Tiger Talisman. Gan-bu-tcha is the same name as Kampuchea. Zhou Da-guan's book mentions the two envoys who were sent to Zhen-la and who did not return, but it does not mention they should be Ali and Chang Tshun. But both were sent by the Java Expedition forces which passed through Champa.

1292 年，毯陽同沒剌予，亦遣使入朝。[7]據[民國]柯邵

---

[5] [明]宋濂等撰，元史，本紀第十七，世祖十四，頁 365。

　　[Ming] Song Lien, et al., *Yuan Shi*(*A History of Yuan Dynasty*), Main Record, No.17, Shi Zu, No.14, in Yang Jialuo(ed.), *op.cit.*, p.365.

[6] 虎符之目的是授予將軍擁有調兵作戰之權力。

　　The purpose of the Tiger Talisman is to entitle power to a general to dispatch and conduct soldiers.

[7] [清]曾廉撰，元書，卷一百，南蕃列傳第七十五，毯陽條，宣統三年撰，文海出版社，台北市，民國 80 年重印，頁 13。

　　[Qing] Zeng Lien, *Yuanshu*(*Book on Yuan*), volume 100, Nan Fan Lie Chuan(Biography of Southern Barbarian), No.75, Dan-young, Xuantong third year(1911), Wenhai Publishing Company, Taipei, 1991 reprint, p.13.

忞撰，新元史之記載，「元貞一年(1295 年)，淡洋一名毯陽，俗淳，男女椎髻，港口通貿易，有大溪之源，二千餘里奔流，合於海，其海水清淡，故名淡洋。」[8] 淡洋，指柬埔寨的洞里薩湖（Tonle Sap Lake）。故淡洋即是指真臘（柬埔寨）。

In 1292, Tang-young and Me-la-yu sent a mission separately to China. According to Ker Sao-min's book, *A New History of Yuan*: "In 1295, Dan-young had another name Tan-young, whose customs were very simple and sincere; the men and women tied a hair-knot on their head, there were trade ports and a very long river over two thousand li flowing along into the sea. Its seawater is light, so it is named Dan-young." Dan-young refers to Tonle Sap Lake, thus it means Zhen-la.

外國使節，包括毯陽的使節到了 1294 年 10 月才允准回國，因為元朝出兵打爪哇，曾下令各國使節已到中國者，因「禁商泛海」而留他們在京師。[9]

Not until October 1294 were the foreign envoys, including Tan-young, allowed to return home, because the Yuan Dynasty attacked Java, and thus ordered the prohibition of sea trade and going abroad. Therefore, the Yuan kept those

---

[8] [民國]柯邵忞撰，新元史，卷之二百五十三，列傳第一百五十，島嶼諸國條，頁 13。

   [Republic of China] Ke Shaomin, *New History of Yuan*, volume 253, biography, No.150, Island countries, p.13.

[9] [明]宋濂等撰，元史，卷十八，本紀第十八，成宗一，頁 382-388。

   [Ming] Song Lien, et al., *Yuan Shi(A History of Yuan Dynasty)*, Main Record, No.18, Cheng Zong, No.1, in Yang Jialuo(ed.), *op.cit.*, pp.382-388.

foreign envoys in the capital of China.

「成宗元貞元年(1295)十一月丙戌，毯陽酋長之兄脫杭捧于奉金表來覲。」[10]

In November 1295, the elder brother of Tan-young's chief came to China and offered a golden paper to the Yuan emperor. After that, there were no offerings again.[11]

從以上元史一書在短短 15 年間之記載可知，真臘有干不昔、甘不察、毯陽，甚至淡洋之不同名稱，足見當時史家對於該國不熟悉，才會出現如此分歧的國名。在該段時間，雖然真臘跟元朝尚有微弱的貿易關係，但其國王並未獲得元朝冊封，亦無固定的貢期，所以難以稱為元朝的朝貢國。因為真臘國王並未獲得元朝冊封，故周達觀記載其國王為國主。占城國王也是未經元朝冊封，一樣稱為國主。

From the above-mentioned book, *A History of Yuan*, we can understand that in a very short time of fifteen years, this book recorded the name of Zhen-la, including Gan-bu-shih, Gan-bu-tcha, and Tan-young, even Dan-young. The historians of that time really didn't know Zhen-la. During that time, Zhen-la had very weak trade relations with the Yuan Dynasty,

---

[10][明]宋濂等撰，元史，卷十八，本紀第十八，成宗一，頁 397。

[Ming] Song Lien, et al., *Yuan Shi*(*A History of Yuan Dynasty*), Main Record, No.18, Cheng Zong, No.1, in Yang Jialuo(ed.), *op.cit.*, p.397.

[11] [清]曾廉撰，元書，卷一百，南蕃列傳第七十五，真臘條，頁 11。

[Qing] Zeng Lien, *Yuanshu*(*Book on Yuan*), volume 100, Nan Fan Lie Chuan(Biography of Southern Barbarian), No.75, Zhen-la, p.11.

but the king didn't get diplomatic recognition and did not receive canonization from the Yuan. Therefore Zhou Da-guan recorded Zhen-la's King as Lord. Similarly, Champa's king is also called Lord.

此外，該書最大疑點為，周達觀係隨從，但書中未提及正使為何人。有違過去史書撰寫習慣，中國歷代遣使都會在正史中記載正使和副使姓名。周達觀在書中僅記載真臘國王風采，但身為使節之隨從，卻未記載正式使節會見真臘國王之過程，誠令人不解和疑惑，因此很可能他為一般商人或是元朝派遣的間諜，目的在探查真臘的虛實，而偽稱為使節。

Besides, there is another big question, namely, Zhou Da-guan is part of a retinue, but he didn't mention the names of the formal envoy and deputy envoy; that is against the custom of the Chinese historical books. Generally, it is necessary to record the names of envoys going to foreign countries. Zhou Da-guan recorded only the elegant demeanor of the King and never recorded the process of a formal envoy seeing the King. That is genuinely puzzling and doubtful. Based on this inference, it is probable that Zhou Da-guan was a businessman or engaged in espionage in order to investigate the national conditions of Zhen-la.

以後至元仁宗延祐七年(1320 年)九月甲辰，元朝遣瑪薩曼（舊作馬札蠻）等使占城、真臘、龍牙門，索馴象。

[12]雙方才又有來往。泰定二年(1325 年)，真臘遣使奉表進
方物。[13]從上述簡史可知，柬埔寨和元朝關係冷淡。

After Zhou Da-guan's mission, the Yuan Dynasty once
again sent Ma-Sa-Man to Champa, Zhen-la, and the Lingga
Islands, to request elephants in September 1320. China
restored trade relations with Zhen-la. And Zhen-la dispatched
a mission to give offerings to China in 1325. From this brief
description, China and Zhen-la kept a very indifferent
relationship.

周達觀在 1297 年 6 月搭船回國，8 月 12 日抵寧波。
他在回國後寫了真臘風土記報告。該書在明朝開始有刻本
出版，因為傳抄的關係，而出現各種版本，雖大同而小異。
本書係根據金榮華於 1976 年出版之真臘風土記校注之版
本而譯為英文。

Zhou Da-guan returned to China in June 1297 and
arrived at Ning-po on August 12. He wrote this book, which
was not published in the Yuan Dynasty but in the Ming
Dynasty. Because of differences in handwriting, this book has
different versions. Whatever the versions are, they are quite

[12] [清]畢沅，續資治通鑑，卷第二百，元紀十八，載於續修四庫全書，
上海古籍出版社，上海市，2002 年，頁 442。
[Qing] Bi Yuan, *Continued Zi Zhi Tong Jian*, Volume 200, Yuan Ji 18,
contained in the *Continuation of Compilation of Siku Quanshu*, Shanghai
Ancient Books Publishing Company, Shanghai, 2002, p. 442.
[13] [清]曾廉撰，元書，卷一百，南蕃列傳第七十五，真臘條，頁 11。
[Qing] Zeng Lien, *Yuanshu(Book on Yuan)*, volume 100, Nan Fan Lie
Chuan(Biography of Southern Barbarian), No.75, Zhen-la, p.11.

similar in general but have differences in a few words only. I base my translation into English on the version of Jīn Rónghuá's *A Correction and Annotation of the Record on the Custom and Land of Zhen-la*, published in 1976.

二、該書的歷史意義
2. Historical Meaning of this Book

　　在此書出版之前的年代，中國古籍對外國之記載，都是透過船員或旅人之口述記錄而成，本書最大的特點是作者親訪所見而寫出的。比該書還早出版 70 多年的趙汝适在 1225 年所撰的諸蕃志，是作者趙汝适擔任海關官員時從來往的船員口中所述記載而成，他自己本人並未親訪東南亞和南亞諸國。

　　Before the time this book was published, most of the Chinese books on foreign countries were written from the oral descriptions of sailors and tourists. The specific trait of Zhou's book is that this is his own personal tour and observation. A book that was published earlier than Zhou's book is Zhào Rǔgua's *Annals on the Various Barbarians*, published in 1225. Zhào Rǔgua was a customs official who recorded the story of overseas voyages of sailors, but he had never by himself gone around to those foreign countries.

　　同樣地，中國文獻對於外國都是僅約略記載其種族和與中國的朝貢關係，對於內政和風俗都是三言兩語，除了越南之外。而本書則是詳細記載真臘的國情和風俗習慣，甚至日常生活都記載詳細。其間亦有記載怪誕的行為及加上他個人的想像和神話故事。如把這一部份除去，全書應有百分九十是可靠的。

Similarly, the race of foreign countries and their tribute relations with China were always recorded in most Chinese historical books. They simply briefly recorded their interior affairs and customs, except for Vietnam. Zhou's book records comprehensively the national conditions, customs, and habits, even the daily life of the Zhen-la people. Among them, there are some weird parts that come from Zhou's imagination. With the exception of those mythological stories, about ninety percent of this book is credible.

本書之所以受到各國之注意，而有數國之譯本，乃因該書是紀錄吳哥城最早的一本著作，連柬埔寨都無該城市寺廟建築的歷史文獻，故極具歷史價值。周達觀前往吾哥城的時間，剛好是吾哥王朝由盛轉衰的時候，它的建築物規模和數量應該也是到最高點。周達觀去的時候，真臘國王是英德拉瓦曼三世（Indravarman III,1295-1307），他是賈亞瓦曼八世（Jayavarman VIII）的女婿，在 1295 年發動政變取得政權。周達觀在他的著作中記載，英德拉瓦曼三世獲得他的妻子的協助，偷取國王的金劍，將陰謀政變的王子逮捕剁去其雙足而取得政權。

This book has received attention and has several different language translations; the important reason is this is the earliest book to record the Angkor architecture groups, for even in Cambodia there are no historical documents on the

Angkor buildings. Zhou's book has historic importance. When Zhou arrived at Angkor, it was the time the Angkor Empire was beginning to decline; its scale of buildings and numbers might have reached a peak. At the time when Zhou was staying at Zhen-la, the King was Indravarman III who was the son-in-law of Jayavarman VIII. King Indravarman III took power by coup in 1295. Zhou's book recorded: "When his father-in-law died, his wife secretly stole the gold sword and gave it to her husband. Consequently, the son couldn't succeed to the throne from his father. He tried to launch a coup, but the new Lord discovered it and chopped off his toes, and imprisoned him in a secluded room."

　　賈亞瓦曼八世信奉濕婆神，也是偶像破壞者，他破壞或修改了許多佛陀造型。在巴揚的許多小佛廟被拆除，改為濕婆神廟。在英德拉瓦曼三世執政時期，小乘佛教成為真臘的國家宗教。[14]在他之後，吾哥城已沒有新建築。所以周達觀所看到的吾哥城建築，應該就是今天所看到的規模。

Jayavarman VIII believed in Shaivism and spoiled a lot of Buddha figures. He tore down many Buddhist temples in Bayon and changed them into Shaivism temples. But with the rule of Indravarman III, who believed in Hinayana Buddhism, it was even enacted as a national religion. After then, there was no new building in Angkor City, so the observations of

---

[14] Dawn F. Rooney, *Angkor, An Introduction to the Temples*, Airphoto International Ltd., Hong Kong, 2002, p. 29.

Zhou should be the scale of what we see nowadays.

　　第二，該書對於國王主持朝政、宮廷裝飾和生活、出入乘轎輿、軍隊、一般百姓之日常家庭生活、服飾、婚姻、婦女生產、宗教、語言文字以及山川動植物出產等，都做了詳細和生動的描述。

　　Secondly, this book described comprehensively and vividly the King presiding over the affairs of state, the decoration of the palace and life in the palace, riding palanquins and carts, the troops, the daily life of ordinary people, clothing, marriage, giving birth to a baby, religion, languages and writing, mountains, rivers, animals, vegetables, products, etc.

　　第三，該書記載僧侶讀佛經是用貝葉疊成的經書。另又記載一件東南亞書寫史的重要紀錄，就是當時柬埔寨人已使用鹿皮作為書寫的工具，人們將鹿皮染成黑色，然後用白粉和水揉成細條，再將之畫在鹿皮上。在此之前，包括柬埔寨和其他東南亞地區都是使用貝多葉（棕櫚葉）書寫。印尼東爪哇和馬都拉島在第十二世紀初葉伊斯蘭教傳進之後，因為阿拉伯字母難以使用貝多葉書寫，故開始轉變使用木板、阿拉伯紙和中國紙。[15]

　　Thirdly, this book recorded that the monks read Buddhist scriptures which were made from palm leaves combined into

---

[15] Theodore G. Th. Pigeaud, *Synopsis of Javanese Literature 900–1900 A.D.*, Springer Science & Business Media, Leiden, Netherlands, 2012, pp. 35-36.

a book. On the other hand, this book also recorded a very important thing, that is, at that time the Cambodians used deer skin to write on. They tinted the deer skin to a black color, and then taking powder, like Chinese white chalk, fashioned the powder into a small stick which was used to write characters on the deer skin. Before this time, Cambodia and other Southeast Asian countries used generally palm leaves to write on. When Islam spread to east Java and Madura Island in the early twelfth century, because Arabic characters were difficult to write on the palm leaves, the people began to use boards, Arabic paper, or Chinese paper.

第四，很多遊客到泰國都知道泰國有人妖秀，已成為泰國吸引觀光客的重要景點。其實在 1980 年代以前，有人妖表演的國家有泰國、馬來西亞和新加坡。新加坡政府在 1980 年取締人妖表演，以致於新加坡已無人妖蹤跡。馬來西亞尚有，但不如泰國有名。人妖源自何國？有不同的說法。真臘風土記有所記載，該書說：「國中多有二形人，每日以十數成群，行於墟場間。常有招徠唐人之意，反有厚饋，可醜可惡。」換言之，男人扮成女人，成為「二形人」，常在市場招攬客人，他們形同阻街女郎。柬埔寨是「二形人」發源地，如今沒落，跟該國長期戰亂有關。

Fourthly, nowadays many tourists have a special experience in Thailand, that is, to watch a "shemale show". It is scarcely recorded in books. Before the 1980s, there were "shemale shows" in Thailand, Malaysia, and Singapore. The government of Singapore prohibited the "shemale show" in

1980. There have been "shemale shows" in Malaysia, but not as famous as in Thailand. Which country is the origin of the "shemale"? There have been different arguments put forth. In Zhou's book, I find a very interesting record, which said: "This country has a lot of two-appearance (a man playing a woman) people who form groups of ten or more persons and engage in business in the market. They are always enticing the Chinese men, even giving them generous feedback. Their behavior is shameful and disgusting." I think these "two-appearance people" is the shemale. They solicit men for sexual transactions in the market. Until now, Cambodia has not used the "shemale show" to solicit tourists, for she has experienced continuingly the ravages of war.

第五，當時的柬埔寨流行三種宗教，周達觀雖寫為儒者（班詰）、僧者（苧姑）和道者（八思惟），其實班詰是指婆羅門教的婆羅門，苧姑是佛教之和尚，八思惟是印度教濕婆派之禁欲主義者。此正符合當時柬埔寨流行的三種宗教，惟小乘佛教日益興盛，其他兩種宗教則漸趨式微。

Fifthly, in Zhou's era, there were three kinds of religions in Cambodia. Zhou Da-guan recorded that they included Ban-Jiea, Ju-Gu, and Ba-Si-Wei. Actually, Ban-Jiea refers to Brahma of Brahmanism, Ju-Gu refers to Buddhist monks, and Ba-Si-Wei refers to ascetics of Shaivism (Hinduism). Zhou's book lets us understand that three kinds of religion existed at that time. Then Hinayana Buddhism was increasingly rising, and the other two religions were going into decline.

16 Record on the Custom and Land of Zhen-la (Chinese v. English Version)

正文

Text

總敍

General Preface

　　真臘國或稱占臘，其國自稱曰甘孛智。今聖朝按西番經，名其國曰澉浦只，蓋亦甘孛智之近音也。

　　白話文(Vernacular)：

　　真臘國或稱占臘，這個國家自稱甘孛智。今聖朝（按指元朝）按西藏佛教經書，稱這個國家為澉浦只，此亦是甘孛智之近音。

　　Zhen-la or Cham-la was called by the Zhen-la people as Cam-bo-chi. Nowadays the Sacred (Yuan) Dynasty called this country as Cam-pu-chi according to Tibet Buddhist scriptures, for it sounds near the pronunciation as Cam-bo-chi.

　　自溫州開洋，行丁未針。歷閩、廣海外諸州港口，過七洲洋，經交趾洋到占城。又自占城順風可半月到真蒲，乃其境也。又自真蒲行坤申針，過崑崙洋，入港。港凡數十，惟第四港可入，其餘悉以沙淺故不通巨舟。然而彌望皆修藤古木，黃沙白葦，倉卒未易辨認，故舟人以尋港為難事。自港口北行，順水可半月，抵其地曰查南，乃其屬郡也。又自查南換小舟，順水可十餘日，過半路村、佛村，渡淡洋，可抵其地曰干傍，取城五十里。

　　白話文(Vernacular)：

從溫州開船，走西南方向。歷經福建、廣東海外諸州港口，過七洲洋，經交趾洋到占城。又自占城順風航行半月可到真蒲，就進入其國境了。又從真蒲走西南西方向，過崑崙洋，進入其港口。它的港口有數十個，惟有第四港可進入，其餘都因泥沙淤淺故不通大船。然而一眼望去，都是修長的藤和老樹、黃沙、白色蘆葦，擋住視線，倉卒未易辨認，故船人尋找港口有困難。從港口向北行，順水半月可抵達查南，是其屬郡也。又從查南換小船，順水航行十餘日，過半路村、佛村，渡過淡洋，可抵達干傍，此地到都城有五十里。

My ship sailed from Wenzhou port and went in a west-southward direction, along the coast of Min (Fújiàn) and Guangdong, passing over the ports without mooring. Passing through Seven Islands Ocean, Chiau-chi Ocean to Champa, and from there to Zhen-pu with a downwind for over half a month. Zhen-pu belongs to Zhen-la. From there sailing in a west-southwest direction, we went through the Kun-lun Ocean and entered into the ports, but the fourth port can be moored; the rest of more than ten ports can't be moored by big ships for they are silted over. Along the banks of the river, there grow many old trees, long vines, yellow sand, and white reeds as far as you can see. The sailors felt that it is difficult to find a place of entrance if you through negligence do not discern the voyage route. Going in a northern direction from this port, with smooth water flow, you can reach Cha-nan County within half a month. And then, from there, you change to take a small boat over ten days with a smooth water flow, sailing past Ban-lu village and Fu village, and crossing over Tonle Sap Lake to get to a place of Gan-bang, fifty li from the capital city.

按諸番志稱其地廣七千里，其國北抵占城半月路，西北距暹半月程，北[16]距番禺十日程，其東則大海也。舊為通商來往之國。

白話文(**Vernacular**)：

按諸番志之記載，稱其地廣七千里，該國北抵占城約半個月的路程，西北距暹國半個月的路程，北距番禺十日的路程，其東則大海也。舊為通商來往之國家。

According to *Annals on the Various Barbarians*, Zhen-la has a wide expanse of land of seven thousand li. Its northern boundary accesses Champa in a distance of half a month by walking, its northwestern boundary to Sien country (Sukhothai Dynasty)[17] takes half a month, and northward to Fan-yu takes ten days; to the east is an ocean. In the past, this country has had commercial relations with China.

---

[16] 原文寫為「南」字，應屬錯誤，蓋番禺位在北方，故改之。

The original text was written as "South", which should be an error. Because Fan-yu is located in the north, so I correct it.

[17] 在中國文獻裡，暹羅指的是阿瑜陀耶王朝，它建立於 1350 年。暹國則是指素可泰王朝，它建立於 1238 年，當周達觀訪問真臘時，暹羅尚未出現。

In Chinese terms, the Sien-lo（暹羅）refers to the Ayudhya Dynasty which was established in 1350. The Sien（暹國）country refers to the Sukhothai Dynasty which was established in 1238. When Chou Da-guan stayed at Zhen-la, the country Siam did not yet exist.

聖朝誕膺天命，奄有四海，唆都元帥之置省占城也，嘗遣一虎符萬戶、一金牌千戶，同到本國，竟為拘執不返。元貞之乙未六月，聖天子遣使招諭，俾余從行。以次年丙申二月離明州，二十日自溫州港口開洋，三月十五日抵占城。中途逆風不利，秋七月始至，遂得臣服。至大德丁酉六月回舟，八月十二日抵四明泊岸。其風土國事之詳，雖不能盡知，然其大略亦可見矣。

白話文(Vernacular)：

聖朝承擔天命，統治四海，唆都元帥在占城設省，曾派遣一虎符萬戶、一金牌千戶，一起至真臘，竟被拘執而沒有回國。元貞之乙未年六月，聖天子遣使招諭，派我從行。在次年丙申年二月離開明州，二十日自溫州港口開航，三月十五日抵達占城。中途遇到逆風不利，秋七月始到達，獲得他們的禮待。至大德丁酉年六月乘船回國，八月十二日抵四明登岸。我詳記該國風土國事，雖不能完全清楚，亦可見其大略。

The sacred Yuan Dynasty received the Mandate of Heaven to hold the four seas. Marshall Sordu leads a Conquer-Champa Moving-Province[18] to attack Champa, and has sent a general who wears a Tiger Talisman and owns the tributes of ten thousand households and a commander who wears a

---

[18] 元國為了攻打占城，設立征占城行省，它代表中央政府的中書省，執行軍事任務，猶如前線軍事指揮部，當戰爭結束後，該征占城行省就裁撤。

In order to attack Champa, the Yuan Dynasty set up a military command which is called Conquer-Champa Moving-Province. It means that the military commander represents the central government conducts the military and administers the affairs in the front war field. When the war ends, it is immediately abolished.

Golden Medal and owns the tributes of one thousand households; both together went to Zhen-la. But the two officials were captured and didn't return. In June 1295, the Yuan emperor sent an envoy to inform Zhen-la to send a mission to China and ordered me to accompany them. The Chinese mission left Ming-chou (Ning-po) in February 1296, departed from Wen-chou on the 20th day, arriving at Champa on March 15th. But we suffered from a headwind and were delayed in Angkor in Autumn July. Consequently, we secured their courtesy treatment. Our ship come back in June 1297 and was anchored at Si-ming (another name for Ning-po) on August 12th. Although I can't record all the national affairs of Zhen-la in detail, it helps to understand its general situation.

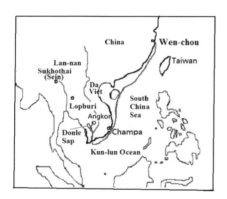

圖 1：周達觀航行至真臘路線圖

Figure 1: Chou Da-guan's voyage route

Sources: Drew by Chen Hurng Yu.

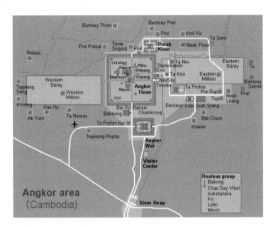

圖 2：吳哥寺平面位置圖

Figure 2: Location of Angkor Architecture Sites

Sources: "Angkor," *Wikipedia*,

http://en.wikipedia.org/wiki/Angkor

1. 城廓
1. The City and Its Walls

　　州城周圍可二十里，有五門，門各兩重。惟東向開二門，餘向皆一門。城之外皆巨濠，濠之上通衢大橋。橋之兩傍共有石神五十四枚，如石將軍之狀，甚巨而獰，五門皆相似。橋之欄皆石為之，鑿為蛇形，蛇皆七頭。五十四神皆以手拔蛇，有不容其走逸之勢。

　　白話文(Vernacular)：

　　州城周圍約有二十里，有五門，各有兩重門。惟東向開二門，餘向皆一門。城之外有巨大的護城河，護城河之上有通衢大橋。橋之兩傍共有石神五十四枚，如石將軍之形狀，甚為巨大而面目猙獰，五門皆相似。橋之欄杆用石頭做成，鑿為蛇形，蛇都是七頭。五十四神皆以手抓蛇，有不容其逃脫之態勢。

The circumference of Angkor Thom city has 20 li, including five gates; each gate has double door plates. In the directions of west, south, and north, there is only one gate each, but the east direction has two gates. Outside of the City-wall, there is a very large moat around the city. Above the moat, there are five big bridges stretching into the city. On both sides of each bridge, there are fifty-four stone gods. They look like stone generals, very huge and fierce-looking. Each gate has the same architectural style. The bridge railing was made of stone in the shape of a carved snake that has seven heads. All those fifty-four stone gods grasp the snake with their hands; it seems that they want to prevent it from escaping.

圖 3：吳哥寺鳥瞰

Figure 3: Angkor Wat Moat

Sources: "Angkor Wat moat drying 'could affect foundations'," *The Phnom Penh Post*, April 1, 2019.

圖 4：吳哥通南城門左右兩側的善惡神頭像

Figure 4: Stone gods grasp a big snake with seven heads in Angkor Thom

Sources: "The City Of The God Kings: Angkor Wat (Ancient Civilizations Documentary) Timeline," https://www.youtube.com/watch?v=KsDGDzwuQ-I

圖 5：吳哥通南城門左側的善神頭像

Figure 5: Kind stone gods grasp a big snake with seven heads on the left side of Angkor Thom South Gate

Sources: "Angkor Thom - Cambodia.mov, "
https://www.youtube.com/watch?v=gkXMpxDuxmw

圖6：吳哥通南城門右側的惡神頭像

Figure 6: Evil stone gods grasp a big snake with seven heads
on the right side of Angkor Thom South Gate

Sources: "Angkor Thom - Cambodia.mov, "
https://www.youtube.com/watch?v=gkXMpxDuxmw

城門之上有大石佛頭三，面向四方。中置其一，飾之
以金。門之兩旁，鑿石為象形。城皆疊石為之，高可二丈。
石甚周密堅固，且不生繁草，卻無女墻。城之上，間或種
桄榔木，比比皆空屋。其內向為坡子，厚可十餘丈。坡上
皆有大門，夜閉早開，亦有監門者，惟狗不許入門。曾受
斬趾刑人亦不許入門。

白話文(Vernacular)：

城門之上有大石佛頭三個，面向四方。中間那個，用
黃金裝飾。門之兩旁，鑿石為象形。城都是使用石塊堆疊
建造，高有二丈。石城甚周密堅固，且不生雜草，但沒有
做女兒牆。城之上，中間或種桄榔木，很多房子是空著。
其內向為坡子，厚可十餘丈。坡上皆有大門，晚上關，早

上開，亦有守門員，惟狗不許入門。曾受斬趾刑的人也不許入門。

On the top of the city gate, there are three stone Buddha heads, facing in four directions. The central one of the heads was decorated with gold. On both sides of a gate, there is a stone carved in the shape of an elephant. The city wall is constructed of piled-up stones about twenty feet high. The stones are very tightly compacted and sturdy, therefore no weeds grow on them. The walls have no battlements. They planted a few scattered palm trees on the top of the city wall, and most of the houses are empty. The inside of the city wall is shaped as a slope; its width is about one hundred feet. There is a big gate on the slopes which is closed at night and opened in the early morning. There is a gatekeeper, who prevents dogs and criminals who have had their toes cut off from entering the city gate.

圖 7：吳哥寺城門上的佛陀像

Figure 7: Buddha on the City-gate
Source:
https://www.pinterest.com/pin/372250725421559480/

其城甚方整，四方各有石塔一座。

白話文(Vernacular)：

此城甚為方整，四方各有石塔一座。

The city wall is shaped like an exact square and in each corner of the four directions, there is a stone tower.

當國之中有金塔一座，傍有石塔二十餘座，石屋百餘間。東向有金橋一所。金獅子二枚，列於橋之左右。金佛八身，列於石屋之下。金塔之北可一里許，有銅塔一座，比金塔更高，望之鬱然。其下亦有石屋數十間。又其北一里許，則國主之廬也。其寢室又有金塔一座焉。所以舶商自來有富貴真臘之褒者，想為此也。

白話文(Vernacular)：

國中有金塔一座，傍有石塔二十餘座，石屋百餘間。東向有金橋一所。金獅子二枚，列於橋之左右。金佛八座，列於石屋之下。金塔之北約一里許，有銅塔一座，比金塔更高，看起來高大的樣子。其下亦有石屋數十間。又其北一里許，則是國主住的房舍。其寢室又有金塔一座。所以外國船商自古以來褒獎真臘之富貴，想就是此原因。

There is a golden tower (Bayon) located in the center of the city, and 20 or more stone towers and one hundred or more houses by its sides. A golden bridge stands in the eastern direction and is decorated with a golden lion on each flank of the bridgehead. There are eight golden Buddhas, lined and mosaicked under the stone house. About one li north of the Golden Tower, there is a copper tower, taller than the Golden Tower and a lofty sight. There are also ten or more stone houses. About one li north, there is the residence of the Lord.[19] Another golden tower is located in his bedroom. This is the reason why the foreign businessmen praised it as "rich Zhen-la".

圖 8：吳哥通的巴揚廟

Figure 8: Bayon, Angkor Thom

Sources:" Bayon. Angkor Thom, Siem Reap Province, Cambodia,"

---

[19] 在中國的習慣，國王未獲中國冊封者，稱之為國主。獲中國冊封者，才能稱為國王。周達觀前往真臘時，真臘國主並未獲得中國冊封。

In Chinese custom, the king of those countries, which did not get recognition and canonized by China, was called the lord. If they are recognized by China, they will have the title of king. When Chou Da-guan stayed at Zhen-la, Zhen-la was not recognized by the Yuan Dynasty.

石塔在南門外半里餘，俗傳魯班一夜造成。魯班墓在南門外一里許，周圍可十里，石屋數百間。

白話文(Vernacular)：

在南門外約半里多有一石塔，俗傳是魯班一夜建造完成。魯班墓在南門外一里許，周圍約有十里，石屋數百間。

It is said that overnight Lu Ban constructed a stone tower which is located half a li beyond the southern gate. There is a Lu Ban Tomb located one li beyond the southern gate, which is surrounded by ten li of land and has several hundred stone houses.

東池在城東十里，周圍可百里，中有石塔、石屋。塔之中有臥銅佛一身，臍中常有水流出。味如中國酒，易醉人。

白話文(Vernacular)：

東池在城東十里，周圍約有百里，中間有石塔和石屋。塔之中央有臥銅佛一座，肚臍中常有水流出。味如中國酒，易使人醉。

The East Pond is located east of about ten li and is

surrounded by an expanse of land of one hundred li, with stone towers and stone houses scattered in it. There is one bronze reclining Buddha within the tower, from whose navel water is always flowing out; it tastes like Chinese wine, and people easily get drunk from drinking it.

北池在城北五里，中有金方塔一座，石屋數間。金獅子、金佛、銅象、銅牛、銅馬之屬，皆有之。

白話文(Vernacular)：

北池在城北五里，中間有金方塔一座，石屋數間。金獅子、金佛、銅象、銅牛和銅馬等都有。

The North Pond is located in the north about five li; one square golden tower is within it, and several stone houses are scattered therein. There is also a golden lion, golden Buddha, bronze elephant, bronze cow, and bronze horse.

2. 宮室
2. Palace Housing

國宮及官舍府第皆面東。國宮在金塔、金橋之北，近北門，周圍可五六里。其正室之瓦以鉛為之；餘皆土瓦，黃色。樑柱甚巨，皆雕畫佛形。屋頗壯觀，修廊複道，突兀參差，稍有規模。其菹事處有金窗櫺，左右方柱，上有鏡約有四五十面，列放於窗之旁。其下為象形。聞內中多有奇處，防禁甚嚴，不可得而見也。

白話文(Vernacular)：

王宮及官舍府第都朝向東方。王宮在金塔、金橋之北面，近北門，周圍約有五、六里。其正室之瓦以鉛做成；餘皆土瓦，黃色。樑柱甚巨大，皆雕畫佛陀造形。屋頗壯觀，有長廊和複雜的走道，突兀參差，稍有規模。其辦公處所有格子狀的金窗子，左右方柱，上有鏡子約有四、五十面，列放於窗子旁邊。其下為象形。聽說內中多有奇處，防禁甚嚴，不可得而見也。

The Lord's Palace and official large buildings are facing the eastern direction. The Lord's Palace is located to the north of the golden tower and golden bridge which is near the north gate, and surrounded by an expanse of land of five to six li. The roof of the main room of the palace is laid in lead, and the other roofs are yellow tile. The columns are very large with carved Buddhas on them. The building looks very spectacular and has long corridors and complicated aisles. It has different housing structures and gives a sense of large scale. There is a golden window lattice[20] in the office room. There are right and left square columns arrayed in the window, about forty to fifty mirrors are hung on the square column, which is nearest the window. On the bottom of the column, there are mosaics of an elephant-shaped sculpture. I heard that there are many wonderful things in the inner palace, but I couldn't see them for they strictly prevented it.

其內中金塔，國主夜則臥其下，土人皆謂塔之中有九

---

20 金窗，指陽光照射所呈現的金黃色窗子。
　　The golden window refers to the golden yellow that the sunlight shines on the window.

頭蛇精,乃一國之土地主也。係女身,每夜則見,國主則先與之同寢交媾,雖其妻亦不敢入。二鼓乃出,方可與妻妾同睡。若此精一夜不見,則番王死期至矣;若番王一夜不往,則必獲災禍。

白話文(Vernacular):

寢宮中有一座金塔,國主夜晚就睡在它的下方,土人皆說塔中有一隻九頭蛇精,它是一國之土地主也。它是女身,每夜才出現,國主則先與它同寢交媾,王后亦不敢入內。蛇精在敲打更二鼓時才離開,國王方可與妻妾同睡。若此精一夜不出現,則番王死期到了;若番王一夜不與蛇精同床,則必遭災禍。

The Lord sleeps at night under the golden tower inside the bedroom. The natives said that there is a nine-headed snake living in the golden tower, who is the lord of the land of the whole nation. The snake spirit appears as a woman and has sex with the Lord every night. Even the queen dares not enter the bedroom. This snake spirit comes out to the bedroom between 9:00-11:00 PM, after then the Lord's wife and concubines can enter the bedroom to sleep with the Lord. If the snake spirit doesn't appear one night, then the time of the death of the Lord will come soon. If the Lord does not meet the snake spirit one night, then he should suffer a disaster.

其次如國戚大臣等屋,制度廣袤,與常人家迥別;周圍皆用草蓋,獨家廟及正寢二處許用瓦。亦各隨其官之等級,以為屋室廣狹之制。其下如百姓之家,止用草蓋,瓦片不敢上屋。其廣狹雖隨家之貧富,然終不敢僭府第制度也。

白話文(Vernacular)：

其次有國戚大臣等人的屋舍，都有規定，與常人家有所區別；周圍皆用茅草蓋屋頂，獨家廟及正寢二處許用瓦。亦各隨其官職之等級，做為屋室大小之建造標準。其下如百姓之住家，僅能用茅草蓋，瓦片不敢上屋。其住屋大小雖依據家之貧富而定，然最終不敢仿效府第規模來建造。

Next, the housing of the Lord's relatives and ministers is quite different from the ordinary people. They are allowed to use the tiles to lay the roof of their family-temple and main living room, but the others use thatch. Regarding the size of housing, it depends upon one's level in the official hierarchy. As for ordinary people, only thatch can be used for their housing and not tiles. The size of the housing of ordinary people could be determined by their wealth, but they dare not emulate the architectural style of the big housing.

3. 服飾
3. Dress

自國主以下，男女皆椎髻袒裼，止以布圍腰。出入則加以大布一條，纏於小布之上。布甚有等級，國主所打之布，有直金三四兩者，極其華麗精美。其國中雖自織布，暹及占城皆有來者，往往以來自西洋者為上，以其精巧而細美故也。

白話文(Vernacular)：

自國主以下，男女皆椎髻及裸上身，僅以布圍在腰間。

出入則加以大布一條，纏於小布之上。布有分等級，國主所打之布，有值金三、四兩者，極其華麗精美。其國中雖能自行織布，暹國及占城皆有進口，往往以來自西洋者為上品，以其精巧而細美的緣故。

From the Lord down, all men and women tie their hair in a knot and their upper body is naked; they only wear a cloth tied around the waist. When they come out, they use a large cloth to cover the small cloth. The clothes have different grades: the Lord's clothes are very gorgeous and beautiful and are worth three to four ounces of gold. Although Zhen-la produces the cloth, it is also imported from Sien country (Sukhothai Dynasty) and Champa. The cloth coming from the West Ocean (India) is always regarded as a better one for its delicateness and refinement.

惟國主可打純花布。頭戴金冠子，如金剛頭上所戴者；或有時不戴冠，但以線穿香花，如茉莉之類，周匝於鬢間。項上戴大珍珠三斤許。手足及諸指上皆帶金鐲，指環上皆嵌貓兒眼睛石。其下跣足，足下及手掌皆以紅藥染赤色。出則手持金劍。

白話文(Vernacular)：

惟國主可打純花布。頭戴金冠子，如金剛神頭上所戴者；或有時不戴冠，但以線穿香花，如茉莉之類，周縈於髮鬢間。項上戴大珍珠三斤許。手足及諸手指上皆帶金鐲，指環上皆嵌貓兒眼睛石。他光腳不穿鞋子，腳及手掌皆以紅藥染成紅色。出來則手持金劍。

Only the Lord can wear a single-color cloth. He wears a

golden crown on his head, which looks like the crown of the Escort God Kin-kong. If he doesn't wear the crown, then he wears a string of fragrant flowers, such as jasmine, tying it in his hair-knot. He wears big pearls weighing about three catties (jin) around his neck. He also wears golden bracelets on his wrists and ankles and rings on his fingers. The rings are mosaicked with cat-eye gemstones. The Lord walks barefoot, with a red pigment to tint his feet and the palms of his hands. He holds a golden sword in his hand when he comes out.

百姓間惟婦女可染手足掌，男子不敢也。大臣、國戚可打疏花布，惟官人可打兩頭花布；百姓間惟婦人可打之。新唐人雖打兩頭花布，人亦不敢罪之，以其暗丁八殺故也。暗丁八殺者，不識體例也。

白話文(Vernacular)：

百姓間唯有婦女可染手足掌，男子不敢也。大臣、國戚可打疏花布，惟官員可打兩頭花布；百姓間只有婦人可打之。新唐人雖打兩頭花布，人亦不敢批評他，認為他是暗丁八殺的緣故。所謂暗丁八殺者，指不識體例也。

Only ordinary females can tint their feet and the palms of their hands; the males dare not to do so. The Lord's relatives and ministers can wear multi-colored cloth. The officials can wear two colored cloth. Only ordinary females can wear two colored cloth. Although newcomers of the Chinese wear two-colored cloth, the people would not criticize them, for they are An-Din-Ba-Sa. The so-called "An-Din-Ba-Sa" refers to those unfamiliar with the customs.

4. 官屬
4. Bureaucrats

　　國中亦有丞相、將帥、司天等官，其下各設司吏之屬，但名稱不同耳。大抵皆國戚為之，否則亦納女為嬪。其出入儀從各有等級。用金轎槓、四金傘柄者為上；金轎槓、二金傘柄者次之；金轎槓、一金傘柄者又次之；止用一金傘柄者，又其次之也。其下者止用一銀傘柄者而已，亦有用銀轎槓者。金傘柄以上官，皆呼為巴丁，或呼暗丁。銀傘柄者，呼為廝辣的。傘皆用中國紅絹為之，其裙直拖地。油傘皆以綠絹為之，裙卻短。

　　白話文(Vernacular)：

　　該國亦設有丞相、將帥、天文等官，其下各設官吏之屬，但名稱不同。大抵都是由國戚擔任，他們大都納妾。其出入儀從各有等級。用金轎槓、四金傘柄者為上；金轎槓、二金傘柄者次之；金轎槓、一金傘柄者又次之；只用一金傘柄者，又其次之也。其下者只用一銀傘柄者而已，亦有用銀轎槓者。金傘柄以上的官員，都稱呼為巴丁，或稱呼暗丁。銀傘柄者，稱呼為廝辣的。傘皆用中國紅絹做的，其裙長拖到地上。油傘皆以綠絹做的，裙子是短的。

In Zhen-la, there are officials, such as the prime minister, generals and the commander-in-chief, astronomer, and so on. There are officials of different names according to the sub-system of administration. Most of those positions are appointed to the relatives of the Lord, and there are always married concubines. The etiquette of the officials when going in and out has different grades. The first grade is taking a palanquin with a golden carrying pole and four umbrellas with golden handles; the second grade is taking a palanquin with a golden carrying pole and two umbrellas with golden handles; the third grade is taking a palanquin with a golden carrying pole and one umbrella with a golden handle; the next grade is taking one umbrella with a golden handle. The next one is taking one umbrella with a silver handle, or taking a palanquin with a silver carrying pole. Those above-mentioned officials with an umbrella with a golden handle are called "Ba-Din" or "An-Din". Those officials with an umbrella with a silver handle are called "Se-La-Der". The umbrella is made of Chinese red silk cloth with a fringe that is long enough to brush the ground. The oil umbrella is made of green silk cloth, but its fringe is shorter.

5. 三教
5. Three Religions

　　為儒者呼為班詰，為僧者呼為苧姑，為道者呼為八思惟。

白話文(Vernacular)：
　　該國稱呼學者為班詰，稱呼僧侶為苧姑，稱呼道士為八思惟。

　　The Confucians are called Ban-Jiea. The monks are called Ju-Gu. The Taoists are called Ba-Si-Wei.

　　班詰不知其所祖，亦無所謂學舍講習之處，亦難究其所讀何書。但見其如常人打布之外，於項上掛白線一條。以此別其為儒耳。由班詰入仕者，則為高上之人，項上之線終身不去。

白話文(Vernacular)：

　　班詰不知其知識是傳自誰，亦無所謂學舍講習之處所，亦難清楚其所讀何書。但見其如常人打布之外，於脖子上掛白線一條。以此顯示他為學者而已。由班詰出身而做官者，則為高上之人，脖子上之線終身不拿掉。

　　Ban-Jiea didn't know who his knowledge came from and has no schoolhouse for teaching, and it is even difficult to know what kind of books they read. I saw that they dress like ordinary people, except that they hung a white cord around their necks. They distinguish themselves in that way as Confucian. If a Ban-Jiea gets an official position, then he becomes a superior man. He will keep the white cord around the neck as long as he is alive.

　　苧姑削髮穿黃，偏袒右肩，其下則繫黃布裙，跣足。寺亦許用瓦蓋，中止有一像，正如釋迦佛之狀，呼為孛賴，穿紅，塑以泥，飾以丹青，外此別無像也。塔中之佛，相貌又別，皆以銅鑄成，無鐘鼓鐃鈸，亦無幢幡寶蓋之類。僧皆茹魚肉，惟不飲酒。供佛亦用魚、肉，每日一齋，皆取辦於齋主之家，寺中不設廚竈，所誦之經甚多，皆以貝葉疊成，極其齊整。於上寫黑字，既不用筆墨，不知其以何物書寫。僧亦有用金銀轎槓、傘柄者，若國主有大政亦咨訪之。卻無尼姑。

白話文(Vernacular)：

苧姑則削髮穿黃色衣服，披在右肩，其下則繫黃布裙，光著腳。佛寺亦許用瓦蓋，寺內只有一像，正如釋迦佛之形狀，稱為孛賴，穿紅衣，用泥塑成，裝飾以丹青，此外沒有別的像。塔中之佛，相貌很特別，皆以銅鑄成，無鐘鼓鐃鈸，亦沒有旗幟、橫幅、大遮陽傘之類。僧皆吃魚、肉，惟不飲酒。供佛亦用魚、肉，每日一齋，皆由齋主供養，寺中不設廚竈，所誦之經甚多，皆以貝葉疊成，極其齊整。上頭寫黑字，既不用筆墨，不知用何物書寫。僧侶亦有用金銀轎槓、傘柄者，若國主有大政要議論，也會咨詢僧侶。國中沒有尼姑。

Ju-Gu shave their hair and wear a yellow cloth with their right shoulder uncovered. They wear a yellow sarong and are barefoot. The roof of a temple is also allowed to be laid with tiles. There is only one Buddha idol within the temple, which is called Bo-Lai. This idol was made of earth and wears a red cloth, painted in many colors. Besides, there are no other idols. The Buddha idols within the pagoda have different faces, which are made of bronze. There are no bells, drums cymbals, and no flags, banners, big parasols, etc. The monks eat fish and meat but do not drink wine. The people pray to offer the fish and meat to the Buddha, and one vegetable dish for each day, all coming from the homes of the almsgivers, so there is no kitchen in the temple. The monks read many scriptures which are made of palm leaves and are piled very neatly. They write black characters on the palm leaves, without using brush and ink. I don't know what the tool is that they use to write.

The monks take also a palanquin with golden and silver carrying poles and umbrellas with golden and silver handles. The Lord would consult them on important national affairs. This country has no nuns.

八思惟正如常人，打布之外，但於頭上戴一紅布或白布，如韃靼娘子罟姑之狀而略低。亦有宮觀，但比之寺院較狹。而道教者，亦不如僧教之盛耳。所供無別像，但止一塊石，如中國社稷壇中之石耳，亦不知其何所祖也。卻有女道士。宮觀亦得用瓦。八思惟不食他人之食，亦不令人見食，亦不飲酒。不曾見其誦經及與人功課之事。

白話文(Vernacular)：

八思惟正如常人，打布之外，在頭上戴一紅布或白布，如韃靼娘子戴罟姑形狀之帽子而略低。亦有宮觀，但比之寺院規模較小。而道教者，亦不如僧教之盛大。所供奉的沒有像，僅有一塊石頭，如中國社稷壇中之石頭，亦不知其傳自何人。卻有女道士。宮觀亦可以用瓦。八思惟不食他人之食物，亦不讓人看見他們吃東西，亦不飲酒。不曾見其誦經及與人作法會之事。

Ba-Si-Wei dresses like an ordinary person and wears a cloth sarong. They wear a red or white cloth on their head which looks like Tartar women wearing a tall Hu-Ku cap, but lower than that. They have Taoist temples, but they are smaller than the pagodas. The Taoists are not as popular as the Buddhists. The Taoists pray only to nothing but a stone which is like an altar stone in the Chinese community. I don't know who it came from. This country has female Taoists. The Taoist temples could lay tiles on the roof. Ba-Si-Wei doesn't eat the offerings of other people and nor let anyone see them eating. They don't drink wine. I don't see them chanting the scriptures, and doing puja with other people.

俗之小兒入學者，皆先就僧家教習，暨長而還俗，其詳莫能考也。

白話文(Vernacular)：

在風俗上，小兒入學者，都先到佛廟學習，長大後還俗，其詳情則未能知曉。

In custom, children attend the temples for study from the monks. When they grow up, they return to the laity. I don't know that in detail.

6. 人物
6. The People

人但知蠻俗，人物粗醜而甚黑，殊不知居於海島村僻及尋常閭巷間者，則信然矣。至如宮人及南棚〈南棚乃府第也。〉婦女多有其白如玉者，蓋以不見天日之光故也。大抵一布纏腰之外，不論男女皆露出胸酥，椎髻跣足。雖國主之妻，亦只如此。

白話文(Vernacular)：

人們只知道當地的風俗，人物粗醜而甚黑，他們已習慣於住在海島偏僻的村子及尋常閭巷之間。至如宮人及住在府第之婦女皮膚多有白如玉者，因為她們不曬陽光的緣故。大抵一布纏腰之外，不論男女皆露出胸酥，紮髮髻，光著腳。雖國主之妻，也是如此。

The people know only their uncivilized customs; they look vulgar, ugly, and very black. They live on an island of the sea and in remote villages, and their activities are in the usual way of street life, so they are used to it. As to the people of the palace and the women of Nan-pon (big housing), they have white skin as jade, because they live in rooms without sunshine. Generally speaking, all the men and women wear a cloth around their waist and expose their chest and breasts, tie a hair-knot on their head, and go barefoot. Even the wives of the Lord are doing so.

　　國主凡有五妻，正室一人，四方四人。其下嬪婢之屬，聞有三五千，亦自分等級，未嘗輕出戶。余每一入內，見番主必與正妻同出，乃坐正室金窗中，諸宮人皆次第列於兩廊窗下，徙倚以窺視，余備獲一見。凡人家有女美貌者，必召入內。其下供內中出入之役者，呼為陳家蘭，亦不下一二千。卻皆有丈夫，與民間雜處，只於頂門之前，削去其髮，如北人開水道之狀，塗以銀硃，及塗於兩鬢之傍，以此為陳家蘭別耳。惟此婦可以入內，其下餘人不可得而入也。內宮之前，多有絡繹於道途間。

　　白話文(Vernacular)：
　　國主共有五妻，正室一人，來自四方的妾四人。其下嬪婢之屬，聽說有三、五千人，亦分有等級，未嘗輕易出戶外。我每次入內，見番主必與正妻同出，乃坐正室金窗中，諸宮人皆次第列於兩廊窗下，倚窗窺視，這是我看見的情景。凡人家有女美貌者，必定會被召入宮內。其下供

宮內出入之役者，稱呼為陳家蘭，亦不下一、二千人。她
們都有丈夫，與民間雜處，只於頂門之前，削去其一片頭
髮，如北人開水道之狀，塗以銀硃，及塗於兩鬢之傍，以
此為陳家蘭之記號。惟此婦女可以入宮內，其下其他人不
可得而入也。她們在內宮之前面，往來於路途間去工作。

The Lord has five wives, one wife, and four concubines
who come from the four directions. It is said that there are
three thousand to five thousand female officials of the palace
and maidservants who have different grades. They can go out
of the palace. Every time I went into the palace, the Lord
would come out with his main wife, and he sat in the main
room near the golden window. I find that the palace's women
stand by rank in two lines along two corridors under the
window. They were peeping at me behind the corridors when
I had the opportunity of being received by the Lord. If there
are beautiful daughters in a family, they should be summoned
into the palace. At the lower level, those who are engaged in
miscellaneous works are called "Chen-Jia-Lan". The number
is one thousand or two thousand. They have husbands. They
lived with other ordinary people, but shaved the hair on their
forehead, looking like the hairstyle of an "open aqueduct" of
the (Chinese) Northerners, and painted it and hair on the
temples with a silver color pigment in order to show that they
are "Chen-Jia-Lan". Only these women can enter the palace,
and those below them can't do so. Those women below the
Chen-Jia-Lan" are bustling and walking on the road to work
in front of the inner palace.

尋常婦女，椎髻之外，別無釵梳頭面之飾。但臂中帶金鐲，指中帶金指環。且陳家蘭及內中諸宮人皆用之。男女身上，常塗香藥，以檀、麝等香合成。家家皆修佛事。

白話文(Vernacular)：

一般婦女，除了椎髻之外，別無髮簪和梳頭面之裝飾。但手臂上戴金鐲，手指上戴金指環。且陳家蘭及宮中諸宮女都戴用。男女身上，常塗香藥，以檀、麝等香合成。家家皆修佛事。

Except for tying a hair-knot on the head, ordinary women do not makeup with hairpins and comb. They wear gold bracelets on their arms and gold rings on their fingers. All the Chen-Jia-Lan" and the women in the palace wear them too. Men and women do always apply perfume on their bodies, which is composed of sandalwood, musk, etc. Every family worships the Buddha.

國中多有二形人，每日以十數成羣，行於墟場間。常有招徠唐人之意，反有厚饋，可醜可惡。

白話文(Vernacular)：

國中多有二形人，每日以數十人為一羣，行於市場間。常有招徠華人之意，反而會給予厚饋，是一醜惡的行徑。

This country has a lot of two-appearance (a man playing as a woman) people who go in groups of ten or more persons and engage in business in the market. They are always enticing the Chinese men, even giving them generous feedback. Their behavior is shameful and disgusting.

圖 9：吳哥寺浮雕上的仕女打扮

Figure 9: Women wear gold bracelets on their arms and gold rings on their fingers.

Sources: *"Baphuon Temple Siem Reap, Cambodia,"* https://www.youtube.com/watch?v=96Aiy0D0VmA

7. 產婦
7. Puerpera

番婦產後，即作熱飯，拌之以鹽，納於陰戶。凡一畫夜而除之。以此產中無病，且收斂常如室女。余初聞而詫之，深疑其不然。既而所泊之家，有女育子，備知其事。且次日即抱嬰兒，同往河內澡洗，尤所怪見。

白話文**(Vernacular)**：

番婦產後，即作熱飯，拌之以鹽，將之置入其陰戶內。經一畫夜將之拿掉。她們認為這樣生產後不會生病，且可收緊其陰道像未出嫁前女孩一樣。我初聞而感到詫異，深為懷疑。後來到所寄宿的家裡，有婦女生子，才知悉此事。

該婦女在生產次日即抱嬰兒，同往河中洗澡，此讓我感到驚奇。

After a woman gives birth to a child, immediately hot cooked rice mixed with salt is then put into her vagina. They take it out after one day and night. This function is to prevent the disease from forming after she gives birth and to shrink her vagina as a virgin. When I first heard it, I was surprised by it. I suspected it, and think it is incredible. A woman of the local family I stayed with just gave birth to a child, so I know this thing. Furthermore, the next day, I saw this woman with the baby going to bathe in the river; I felt it is very amazing.

又每見人言：番婦多淫，產後一兩日，即與夫合。若丈夫不中所欲，即有買臣見棄之事。若丈夫適有遠役，只數夜則可，過十數夜，其婦必曰：「我非是鬼，如何孤眠？」淫蕩之心尤切。然亦聞有守志者。婦女最易老，蓋其婚嫁產育既早，二三十歲人，已如中國四五十歲人矣。

白話文(Vernacular)：

又每次聽人說：番婦多淫，產後一兩日，即與夫同床。若丈夫不能滿足其妻之欲望，即有朱買臣被拋棄之事情發生。若丈夫剛好到遠方作戰，只數夜尚可，若超過十數夜，其婦必說：「我不是鬼，如何能一個人睡覺呢？」淫蕩之心尤其急切。然亦聽說有守節者。婦女最容易老，蓋其婚嫁產育既早，二、三十歲的人，看起來已像中國四、五十歲的人了。

I heard that the people said the local women are very prurient; one or two days after they have given birth, they are immediately having sex with their husband. If the husband can't satisfy his wife's desire, he will be abandoned right away, just as in Chu Mai-chen's story. If the husband happened to go far away to engage in a war, it will be all right for a few nights, but if it is over ten nights, his wife would say: "I am not a ghost, how can I sleep alone?" Her lustful mind emerges so urgently. However, there are some women who persist in loyalty to their husbands. The local women easily get old, for they are early to get married and give birth. When they are grown up to twenty or thirty years old, they look like a Chinese woman who is forty or fifty years old.

圖 **10**：吳哥寺浮雕上的生子場景
Figure 10: The birth of a baby
Sources: "The Bayou," *Tien Chiu*,
http://www.tienchiu.com/travels/cambodia/the-ruins-of-angkor/the-bayon/
Note: Second on the right is puerpera.

8. 室女

8. Unmarried Girl

人家養女，其父母必祝之曰：「願汝有人要，將來嫁千百箇丈夫。」富室之女，自七歲至九歲；至貧之家，則止於十一歲，必命僧道去其童身，名曰陣毯。

白話文**(Vernacular)**：

人家養女，其父母必祝賀說：「願妳將來有人要，將來嫁千百個丈夫。」富室之女兒，從七歲至九歲；貧窮之家，則到十一歲，必命僧道去其處女身，名曰陣毯。

The parents of any family that has a daughter would wishfully say to her: "We hope someone wants you, and you will marry several hundreds of thousands of husbands in the future." As for the daughter of a rich family, when grown up to seven or nine years of age, and the daughter of a poor family, when grown up to eleven years of age, their parents would ask a monk or Taoist to take away her virginity, which is called "Tzen-tan".

蓋官司每歲於中國四月內，擇一日頒行本國應有養女當陣毯之家，先行申報官司。官司先給巨燭一條，燭間刻畫一處，約以是夜遇昏點燭，至刻畫處，則為陣毯時候矣。先期一月，或半月，或十日，父母必擇一僧或一道，隨其何處寺觀，往往亦自有主顧。向上好僧皆為官戶富室所先，貧者亦不暇擇也。富貴之家，饋以酒、米、布帛、檳榔、銀器之類，至有一百擔者，直中國白金二三百兩之物。少者或三四十擔，或一二十擔，隨其家之豐儉。所以貧人之家至十一歲而始行事者，為難辦此物耳。富家亦有捨錢與貧女陣毯者，謂之做好事。蓋一歲之中，一僧止可御一女，僧既允受，更不他許。

白話文**(Vernacular)**：

官方每年於中國曆法四月內，擇一日頒行本國應有養女當陣毯之家，先行申報官方。官方先給巨燭一條，蠟燭上刻畫一處，約以是夜昏暗時點燃蠟燭，燒至刻畫處，則為陣毯之時候。在陣毯前一月，或半月，或十日，父母必擇一僧或一道，他們會到僧侶或道士所住之寺觀，選擇其中意之僧侶或道士。向上好僧皆為官家富室所優先選擇，貧者則沒有機會選擇。富貴之家，會回饋以酒、米、布帛、檳榔、銀器之類給僧侶或道士，至有一百擔者，價值中國白金二、三百兩之物。少者或三、四十擔，或一、二十擔，隨其家財富之多寡而定。所以窮人之家至十一歲而始行陣毯者，主因就是難辦此物。富家亦有捐錢給貧女陣毯者，稱為做好事。蓋一年之中，一名僧侶只可為一女做陣毯，僧侶既然允許接受一女，就不可答應他女。

The officials choose one day in April of the Chinese calendar as the stipulated day for the whole country; those families having daughters must report to the officials in advance for being a "Tzen-tan" family. The officials first give a large candle and mark a sign on the candle. They meet one day and wait for nightfall to light the candle, and when it burned to the place of the mark, it is the time for "Tzen-tan". One month, or half a month, or ten days before the "Tzen-tan", the parents should select one monk or one Taoist. They will go to the temple where the monk lives and choose the monk they like. High-ranking and good monks are to be selected in advance by the official and rich families, while the poor families have no opportunity to select. The rich and noble families feed the monk with wine, rice, cloth, areca, silverware, etc. Those gifts weigh as much as one hundred piculs or are worth two or three hundred ounces of Chinese white gold. Some of them give a smaller amount, weighing about thirty or forty piculs, or give even less about ten or twenty piculs. It depends upon the amount of wealth of the family. Thus, the daughters of poor families that are eleven years old can't hold the "Tzen-tan" because it is difficult for them. The rich families also contribute money to the poor families who are doing "Tzen-tan" with their daughters. This is to be called "doing good things". The monk can only do "Tzen-tan" with one girl in a year. If he accepts one, then he can't promise another one.

是夜，其家大設飲食、鼓樂，會親隣。門外縛一髙棚，裝塑泥人、泥獸之屬於其上，或十餘，或止三四枚，貧家則無之。各按故事，凡七日而始撤。既昏，以轎傘鼓樂迎此僧而歸。以綵帛結二亭子，一則坐女於其中，一則僧坐其中，不曉其口説何語。鼓樂之聲喧闐，是夜不禁犯夜。聞至期與女俱入房，親以手去其童，納之酒中。或謂父母親隣各點於額上，或謂俱嘗以口，或謂僧與女交媾之事，或謂無此。但不容唐人見之，所以莫知其的。至天將明時，則又以轎傘鼓樂送僧去。後當以布帛之類與僧贖身。否則此女終為此僧所有，不可得而他適也。余所見者，大德丁酉之四月初六夜也。

白話文(Vernacular)：

這一夜，女子家裡大設飲食、鼓樂，會親友隣居。門外建一高棚，裝塑泥人、泥獸之類於其上，或十餘個，或三、四個，貧家則沒有這些東西。每家作法不同，有七日始裁撤。到了黃昏，以轎傘鼓樂迎僧侶到家。以綵帛連結二轎子，女坐於其中一轎，僧侶坐另一轎，我不曉得他們口説何話。鼓樂之聲喧鬧，當局允許整夜喧鬧。時間到了，僧侶與女都入房內，僧侶親以手去除該女之童貞，將血納之酒中。有的說是請父母親友隣居各點於額上，或有的說大家都嚐一小口，或有的說僧侶與女交媾之事，或說沒有此事。但這些儀式都不容許華人看見，所以不知其詳情。到天將亮時，則又以轎傘鼓樂送僧侶回去。後該女父母以布帛之類向該僧侶贖回女兒身。否則此女終身為此僧侶所有，不能嫁給別人。我所看見此事，是在大德丁酉年四月初六夜。

On the same evening, the family prepares the food, and drumming music, and invites the neighbors to join the banquet. They construct a tall scaffolding outside the house and put clay figurines of people and animals on it. The number of clay figurines is about ten or more, or for a poor family only three or four, nothing more. How long the celebration will last depends upon each family, generally about seven days. At nightfall, the family welcomes the monk with a palanquin, umbrella, and drumming music into the house. They build two pavilions with colorful ribbons. The girl sits inside one, the monk inside the other one. I don't know what they talk about. The drumming sound is very loud, and the authorities allow the noise all night. When the time is up, the monk and the girl together enter into the room. The monk takes away this girl's virginity with his hand and then puts the girl's blood into the wine. There are different sayings that the girl's parents, relatives, or neighbors mark their forehead with a dot of the blood wine with their hand, or taste it in their mouth, or the monk has sex with the girl or nothing happens. Anyway, they don't like the Chinese to watch this process, so I don't really know. At dawn, they see the monk off with a palanquin, umbrella, and drumming music. After that, the parents must pay a redemption of cloth to the monk, otherwise, their daughter will be owned by the monk and can't marry someone else. This is what I saw on the night of April 6, Da-de Year (in 1297).

前此父母必與女同寢，此後則斥於房外，任其所之，無復拘束提防之矣。至若嫁娶，則雖有納幣之禮，不過苟簡從事。多有先姦而後娶者，其風俗既不以為恥，亦不以為怪也。陣毯之夜，一巷中或至十餘家，城中迎僧道者，交錯於途路間，鼓樂之聲，無處無之。

白話文(Vernacular)：

在此之前父母必與女同寢，此後則要她睡在房外，任何地方均可，不再給予拘束或提防。至若嫁娶，則雖有納幣之禮，不過都是簡單從事。多有先發生性關係而後娶者，其風俗既不以為恥，亦不以為奇怪。陣毯之夜，一街巷中有十餘家舉辦，城中迎僧侶或道士者，在路上交錯而行，鼓樂之聲，到處都聽得到。

Before the celebration, the parents sleep together with their daughters, afterwards, she is excluded from her parents' room and goes where she wants without any restraint or guard. As to the marriage, although they have the etiquette of a betrothal gift, it is held with simplicity and austerity. Many people have sex before marriage; they don't feel that such a custom is a shame or a strange thing. On the night of the "Tzen-tan", there are ten or more families in the same lane, and the processions of welcoming the monk or Taoist shuttled in the way of the city. We can hear the sound of the drumming music everywhere.

9. 奴婢
9. Slaves

　　人家奴婢,皆買野人以充其役,多者百餘,少者亦有一二十枚,除至貧之家則無之。蓋野人者,山中之人也。自有種類,俗呼為撞賊。到城中,皆不敢出入人之家,城間人相罵者,一呼之為撞,則恨入骨髓,其見輕於人如此。少壯者一枚可直百布,老弱者止三四十布可得。只許於樓下坐臥。若執役,方許登樓,亦必跪膝合掌頂禮而後敢進。呼主人為巴馳,主母為米。巴馳者父也,米者母也。若有過,撻之,則俯首受杖,略不敢動。

　　白話文(Vernacular):
　　人家之奴婢,都買野人來役使,多者百餘人,少者亦有一、二十人,但至貧之家則沒有。所謂野人者,是山中之人也。他們是特有種類,俗稱呼「為撞」賊。到城中,皆不敢出入人之家，城間人彼此相罵者，若稱呼對方為「為撞」，則恨入骨髓，足見其被人所輕視之程度。少壯的奴婢一個人可價值百布，老弱者只值三、四十布。只許於樓下坐臥。若執行工作，方許登樓，亦必跪膝合掌頂禮而後敢進屋內。呼主人為「巴馳」，主母為「米」。「巴馳」者父也，「米」者母也。若有過失，會遭鞭打，則俯首受杖，動都不敢動。

The family's slaves are bought from barbarians for the purpose of serving. The number of slaves in a family may be one hundred or more, and as few as ten to twenty; the poorest families have none at all. The barbarians come from the mountains, a specific race by themselves. Generally, they are called "Wei Zhuang" thieves. When they come to the city, they dare not go in or out of the house of other people. If a quarrel happens between two city dwellers, they always call the counterpart as "Wei Zhuang". It shows that they hate the counterpart to the marrow of his bones. They are so despised in this way. A young and strong slave is worth a hundred pieces of cloth; the old and weak are only worth thirty to forty pieces of cloth. Generally, the slaves are permitted to sit and sleep on the ground floor. If they need to carry out work, they can go upstairs and must kneel down, fold their palms and bow their head to the ground, and then do the work. They call their master as "Ba-tuo", and their hostess as "Mi". "Ba-tuo" means father, and "Mi" means mother. If they do something wrong, they bow their head and receive a whipping, never moving their body.

其牝牡者自相配偶，主人終無與之交接之理。或唐人到彼久曠者不擇，一與之接，主人聞之，次日不肯與之同坐，以其曾與野人接故也。或與外人交，至於有姙養子，主人亦不詰問其所從來。蓋以其所不齒，且利其得子，仍可為異日之奴婢也。

白話文(Vernacular)：

奴婢之男女自相配偶，主人不會與他們發生性關係。或華人到彼久未與女性發生性關係者，不加選擇，一旦與他們發生性關係，主人聽到，次日不肯與他同坐，以其曾與野人性交的緣故。奴婢若與外邊的人性交，以致於懷孕生子，主人亦不會詰問小孩從何處來。因為他不齒去問，而且可從該小孩得利，仍可做為異日之奴婢也。

The males and females look for their spouses among themselves; the master has no reason to have sexual intercourse with them. A Chinese who came to Zhen-la for a long time had had no sex with a woman; once he had sex with a female slave. When the master heard this news, he would not sit with him the next day because he had sex with a barbarian. Or if a female slave had sex with an outsider, or even gave birth to a child, the master also would never ask where the child came from. Though the master despises the female slave, he will get a profit from this child, who can become his slave in the future.

或有逃者，擒而復得之，必於面刺以青，或於項上帶鐵鎖以錮之，亦有帶於臂腿間者。

白話文**(Vernacular)**：

奴婢有逃跑者，被抓回來後，必於面上刺青，或於脖子上帶鐵鎖以禁錮，亦有鎖在臂和腿者。

Sometimes the slaves escape. When they are captured, they must have a green tattoo put on their face or wear an iron lock around their neck, or tie an iron chain on their arms or legs.

10. 語言
10. Language

國中語言，自成音聲，雖近而占城、暹人，皆不通話說。如以一為梅，二為別，三為卑，四為般，五為孛藍，六為孛藍梅，七為孛藍別，八為孛藍卑，九為孛藍般，十為答呼。呼父為巴駝，至叔伯亦呼為巴駝。呼母為米，姑、姨、嬸姆以至鄰人之尊年者，亦呼為米。呼兄為邦，姊亦呼為邦。呼弟為補溫。呼舅為吃賴，姑夫、姊夫、姨夫、妹夫亦呼為吃賴。

白話文**(Vernacular)**：

國中語言，自成音聲，雖接近占城和暹人的語音，但不能通話。如以一為梅，二為別，三為卑，四為般，五為孛藍，六為孛藍梅，七為孛藍別，八為孛藍卑，九為孛藍般，十為答呼。稱父為巴駝，至叔伯亦稱為巴駝。稱母為米，姑、姨、嬸姆以至鄰人之年長者，亦稱為米。稱兄為邦，姊亦稱為邦。稱弟為補溫。稱舅為吃賴，姑夫、姊夫、姨夫、妹夫亦稱為吃賴。

The language of Zhen-la has a special pronunciation.

Even though it is close to that in Champa and Sien countries, they still can't communicate with each other. For example, one is called "Mei"; two is "Biea"; three is "Bei"; four is "Ban"; five is "Bor-Lan", six is " Bor-Lan-Mei"; seven is "Bor-Lan-Biea"; eight is "Bor-Lan-Bei"; nine is "Bor-Lan-Ban"; ten is "Da-Hu". They call their father as "Ba-Tuo", and their uncle also called Ba-Tuo". They call their mother as "Mi", their aunt and aged neighbors also are called "Mi". They call their elder brother as "Bang", and elder sister also called "Bang". They call young brother as "Bu-Win", and mother's brothers as "Tze-Lai". Husbands of one's father's sister, an elder sister's husband, a husband of one's mother's sister, and a young sister's husband are also called "Tze-Lai".

　　大抵多以下字在上，如言此人乃張三之弟，則曰補溫張三。彼人乃李四之舅，則曰吃賴李四。又如呼中國為備世，呼官人為巴丁，呼秀才為班詰。乃呼中國官人，不曰備世巴丁，而曰巴丁備世。呼中國之秀才，不曰備世班詰，而曰班詰備世。大抵皆如此，此其大略耳。至若官府則有官府之議論，秀才則有秀才之文談，僧道自有僧道之語說。城市村落，言語各自不同，亦與中國無異也。

白話文(Vernacular)：

　　大抵多以後面的詞放在前面，如說此人乃張三之弟，則曰補溫張三。彼人乃李四之舅，則曰吃賴李四。又如稱中國為備世，稱官人為巴丁，稱秀才為班詰。乃稱中國官人，不說備世巴丁，而說巴丁備世。稱中國之秀才，不說備世班詰，而說班詰備世。大抵皆如此，此其大略情況。

至若官府則有官府之議論，秀才則有秀才之文談，僧道自有僧道之話語。城市村落，言語各自不同，亦與中國沒有差別。

Generally, they put the latter word in front; for example, if he is the young brother of Chang San, thus they call him Bu-Win Chang San; and if he is the uncle of Li Si, thus they call him Tze-Lai Li Si. Furthermore, they call China as "Bei-Shi", the officials as "Ba-Din", and a scholar as "Ban-Jiea". Therefore, they call Chinese officials as "Ba-Din-Bei-Shi" rather than "Bei-Shi Ba-Din"; they call Chinese scholars as "Ban-Jiea-Bei-Shi " rather than "Bei-Shi-Ban-Jiea". This is the general condition. As to officials, they have their own bureaucrat discussions, the scholars have their own literate conversations, and the monks and Taoists also have their own languages. Whether in the city or village, all have their respective language. It seems like China.

11. 野人
11. Barbarians

野人有二種：有一等通往來話言之野人，乃賣與城間為奴之類是也；有一等不屬教化，不通言語之野人，此輩皆無家可居，但領其家屬巡行於山，頭戴一瓦盆而走。遇有野獸，以弧矢摽槍射而得之，乃擊火於石，共烹食而去。其性甚狠，其藥甚毒，同黨中人常自相殺戮。近地亦有以種荳蔻、木綿花、織布為業者，布甚粗厚，花紋甚別。

白話文(Vernacular)：

　　野人有二種：有一種通往來言語之野人，乃賣與城間為奴之類；有一種不屬教化，不通言語之野人，此輩皆無家可住，但領其家屬在山區流連，頭戴一瓦盆而走。遇有野獸，以弓矢或標槍射而得之，擊石點火，共同烹食，然後離去。其性甚狠，其藥甚毒，同類中人常自相殺戮。近郊地區亦有以種荳蔻、木綿花、織布為業者，布甚粗厚，花紋很特別。

　　There are two kinds of barbarians: one can communicate with the general language, and they are the slaves sold to the city; the other ones are not educated and can't communicate with the people and are homeless. The uneducated barbarians always take their family with them traversing in the mountains and wearing a clay pot on their head as they walk. When they come across an animal, they shoot it with an arrow or javelin. After catching it, they make a fire by striking stones. They cook and eat together, and then leave for another place. Their nature is very relentless, and their drugs for killing animals are very poisonous. They are always killing one another. Some of them who live close to the city plant cardamom and kapok, and weave cloth for a living. But the cloth is very crude and thick, yet its pattern and design are very special.

12. 文字
12. Writing

　　尋常文字及官府文書，皆以麂、鹿皮等物染黑，隨其大小闊狹，以意裁之。用一等粉，如中國白堊之類，搓為小條子，其名為梭。拈於手中，就皮畫以成字，永不脫落。用畢則插於耳之上。字跡亦可辨認為何人書寫，須以濕物揩拭方去。

白話文(Vernacular)：

尋常文字及官府文書，皆以麂、鹿皮等物染黑，隨其大小寬窄，以自己的意思裁剪。用一種粉，如中國白堊之類，搓為小條子，其名為梭。拈於手中，就皮上書寫成字，永不脫落。用完就插於耳朵上。字跡亦可辨認為何人書寫，可用濕物揩拭擦去。

The general character and official script are written on the skin of muntjak and deer. The method is to tint the deer's skin to a black color and cut it to the size you want. Then, taking a powder, like Chinese white chalk, is rubbed into a small stick which is called "suo". The people hold the "suo" with their fingers to write a character on the skin, and the word appears and will not disappear. When they finished the writing, they place the chalk on their ear. From the handwriting, it can be recognized who wrote the words. Those words can be erased by using a wet material.

大率字樣，正似回鶻字。凡文書皆自後書向前，卻不自上書下也。余聞之也先海牙云，其字母音聲，正與蒙古音聲相類，但所不同者三兩字耳。初無印信，人家告狀，亦無書鋪書寫。

白話文(Vernacular)：

大體上，其文字樣子很像回鶻字。凡文書皆自後向前寫，不是自上而下寫。我聽也先海牙說，其字母音聲，正與蒙古音聲相類，但所不同者三兩字罷了。初期沒有印信，人家告狀，亦沒有書鋪寫狀紙。

In general, the shape of the script looks like Uighur's writing. The writing is from left to right, not from upper to bottom. I heard from Ye-Siam-Hai-Ya who said that the pronunciation of the Zhen-la language is just like the sound of the Mongolian language, from which only two or three words are different. The Zhen-la people didn't use seals. Even when suing in court, there are also no writing agents to write the complaint document.

13. 正朔時序
13. New Year and the Sequence of Seasons

每用中國十月以為正月。是月也，名為佳得。當國宮之前，縛一大棚，棚上[21]可容千餘人，盡掛燈毬花朵之屬。其對岸遠離二三十丈地，則以木接續縛成高棚，如造搭樣竿之狀，可高二十餘丈。每夜設三四座，或五六座，裝煙火爆杖於其上，此皆諸屬郡及諸府第認直。遇夜則請國主出觀，點放煙火爆杖，煙火雖百里之外皆見之。爆杖其大如砲，聲震一城。其官屬貴戚，每人分以巨燭檳榔，所費甚夥，國主亦請奉使觀焉。如是者半月而後止。

白話文(Vernacular)：

---

[21] 原文寫為「上」，不合常理，應是在棚下容納一千多人，故改之。
The original text was written as "upper", which is unreasonable. It should accommodate more than 1,000 people under the shed, so I correct it.

該國以中國曆法十月為正月。是月也，名為佳得。在王宮之前，建一大棚，棚下可容千餘人，掛滿了燈毬花朵之類。其對岸遠離二、三十丈之地方，則以木接續綁成高棚，像建造搭樣竿（鷹架）之形狀，高約二十餘丈。每夜設三、四座，或五、六座，在上頭裝煙火爆杖，此皆諸屬郡及諸府第認捐。一到晚上，則請國主出來觀賞，點放煙火爆杖，煙火雖百里之外皆可看到。爆杖其大如砲，聲震一城。其官屬貴戚，每人分給巨燭和檳榔，所費甚多，國主亦請外國使節觀賞。這樣舉辦半個月才停止。

Zhen-la adopted the tenth month of the Chinese calendar as their first month. They called this month as "Jia-De". In front of the palace, they build up a large shed that can accommodate one thousand or more people and hung up many lanterns and flowers. On the opposite shore, about the distance of two or three hundred feet, they build up a tall scaffolding binding it to log by log, which takes the shape of a tower and stands two hundred feet high. Every night they install fireworks and firecrackers on the top of three or four scaffoldings, five or six scaffoldings; all these facilities are contributions coming from counties and big houses. At night, they invite the Lord to watch and light the fireworks and firecrackers. The fireworks can be seen a hundred li away. The size of the firecrackers is as big as a canon, and the sound of the explosion shakes the whole city. The Lord gives every official and relative a large candle and areca, which costs a lot. The Lord also invites foreign envoys to attend and watch. Such a festival continues for half a month.

每一月必有一事，如四月則拋毬，九月則壓獵。壓獵者，聚一國之象，皆來城中，教閱於國宮之前。五月則迎佛水，聚一國遠近之佛，皆送水來與國主洗身。陸地行舟，國主登樓以觀。七月則燒稻，其時新稻已熟，迎於南門外，燒之以供佛。婦女車象，往觀者無數，國主卻不出。八月則挨藍，挨藍者，舞也。點差伎樂，每日就國宮內挨藍，且鬥豬、鬥象，國主亦請奉使觀焉，如是者一旬。其餘月分，不能詳記也。

白話文(Vernacular)：

每一個月必有一項節慶，如四月則拋毬，九月則壓獵。壓獵者，聚一國之象來城中，於王宮前校閱。五月則迎佛水，聚一國遠近之佛，皆送水來給國主洗身。陸地行舟，國主登樓觀賞。七月則燒稻，其時新稻已熟，在南門外迎接，燒之以供佛。婦女、車子和大象，聚集前往觀賞者無法計數，國主卻不出來。八月則挨藍，挨藍者，跳舞也。選擇舞者，每日到王宮內跳舞，且鬥豬、鬥象，國主亦請外國使節觀賞，如是的慶典連續十天。其餘月分，不能詳記其情況。

Every month has a festival, for example, there is a throwing-ball game in April; Ya-la in September. So-called "Ya-La", means gathering together the elephants of the whole country which come to the city to parade in front of the palace. There is a "welcoming the Buddha (saint) waters" in May, in which the Buddhas far and near gather together to send the waters to the Lord for bathing. The Lord ascends a tower to watch a program on "Boating on land". There is a "burning rice straw" in July. At that time the new rice is already ripe for harvesting, it is welcomed outside the south gate, and then the rice straw is burned as an offering to the Buddha. Many women, chariots, and elephants, gather together to watch, but the Lord is absent. There is "Ai-Lan" in August. The so-called "Ai-Lan" means dancing. They select the dancers to perform daily in the palace. There also is pig-fighting and elephant-fighting, and again the Lord invites the foreign envoys to watch. The festivals continue for ten days. The events of other months, I can't record in detail.

國中人亦有通天文者，日月薄蝕，皆能推算，但是大小盡卻與中國不同。中國閏歲，則彼亦必置閏，但只閏九月，殊不可曉。一夜只分四更。每七日一輪。亦如中國所謂開、閉、建、除之類。番人既無名姓，亦不記生日。多有以所生日頭為名者，有兩日最吉，三日平平，四日最凶。何日可出東方，何日可出西方，雖婦女皆能算之。十二生肖亦與中國同，但所呼之名異耳。如呼馬為卜賽，呼雞為鑾，呼豬為直盧，呼牛為箇之類。

白話文(Vernacular)：
國中人亦有通天文者，他們可以推測日食和月食，但是月的大小卻與中國不同。中國閏歲，則彼亦必置閏，但只閏九月，不知其為何如此。一夜只分四更。每七日一輪。亦如中國所謂開、閉、建、除之類。番人既無名姓，亦不記生日。多有以所生之日子取名的，以每月第二天最吉，每月第三天平平，每月第四天最凶。何日可向東方走，何日可向西方走，雖婦女皆能推算。十二生肖亦與中國同，但所稱呼之音不同。如稱馬為卜賽,稱雞為蠻,稱豬為直盧,稱牛為箇之類。

In this country some people understand astronomy, and they can surmise an eclipse of the sun and the moon. But the long or short of a month is completely different from China's. In China, there is an intercalary year, but in this country, there is only an intercalary ninth month; I really don't know why. They divide the night into four segments (Chinese have five segments), and there is a rotation every seven days. It seems like the open, close, set-up, and repeal in China. The natives have neither family names nor given names, nor remember their birthdays. Many people are named after the day of birth, the second day of each month is the most auspicious, the third day is ordinary, and the fourth day is the most unlucky. As for a day on which they can go to the east or go to the west, even the women can deduce it. They have also twelve calendar animals like China but with different pronunciations. For example, they called the horse as "Bu-Sai", chicken as "Mán", pig as "Zhi-Lu", cow as "Ge", etc.

14. 爭訟
14. Arbitration of Disputes

民間爭訟,雖小事亦必上聞國主。初無笞杖之責,但聞罰金而已。其人大逆重事,亦無絞斬之事。止於城西門外掘地成坑,納罪人於內,實以土石,堅築而罷。其次有斬手足指者,有去鼻者。但姦與賭無禁。姦婦之夫或知之,則以兩柴絞姦夫之足，痛不可忍。竭其資而與之，方可獲免。然裝局欺騙者亦有之。

白話文(Vernacular)：

民間爭訟，雖小事亦必向國主申訴。初期無笞杖之刑，只有罰金而已。若犯下大逆重罪，也沒有絞斬之刑。僅是在城西門外掘坑，將罪人放入坑內，外以土石掩埋半身，予以夯實，就這樣罷了。其次有斬手足指者，有削去鼻子者。但通姦與賭博沒有禁止。姦婦之夫如果知道了，則以兩木頭絞姦夫之腳，痛不可忍。姦夫要拿出其所有財產給予對方，方可獲免。然設局欺騙者亦有之。

Ordinary people for disputes about a small thing would make a petition to the Lord. I heard first this country has no whipping or beating punishments but fines money. If a person commits a serious crime, he would not be punished by death by beheading or hanging. But he will be buried in a hole outside the west gate of the city, and solidly cover his body with the earth and stones; that is at all. Next, there are fingers and toes-cutting, and nose-cutting. There is no prohibition for adultery and gambling. But if a husband knows his wife is having a misconduct with her lover, he uses two sticks to wring the feet of the lover, to make him unbearable. Not until the lover pays what property he owns, can it be resolved consequently. However, there is also setting up cheating to defraud people.

人或有死於門首者，則自用繩拖置城外野地，初無所謂體究檢驗之事。

白話文(Vernacular)：

若有人死在自家門口者，就用繩子拖該屍體到城外野地，初期並無所謂驗屍之事。

If someone dies in front of a home, the homeowner uses a rope to pull the corpse to the wildland outside the city. There is no autopsy.

人家若獲盜，亦可施監禁拷掠之刑。卻有二項可取。且如人家失物，疑此人為盜，不肯招認，遂以鍋煎油極熱，令此人伸手於中；若果偷物，則手腐爛，否則皮肉如故。云番人有異法如此。

白話文(Vernacular)：

一般人若抓獲盜賊，亦可施予監禁拷打之刑。卻有二項值得注意，假如人家失物，懷疑此人為盜，不肯招認，就以鍋煎油極熱，令此人將手伸入鍋中；如果他偷物，則手會腐爛，否則皮肉如以前一樣完好。讓人驚訝番人有此特異法律。

If a person arrests a thief, he can impose the punishments, such as detention, torture, or beating. There are two things worthy of notice. The first one is that if a person loses something and suspects someone stole it, but that person refuses to admit it, then an arbitrator can heat up oil, and ask the suspect to put his hand into the pot of oil. If the suspect really stole the things, then his hand would rot away; otherwise, the skin and flesh would remain the same as before. What a surprise these barbarians keep these strange laws.

又兩家爭訟，莫辨曲直。國宮之對岸有小石塔十二座，令二人各坐一塔中。塔之外，兩家自以親屬互相隄防。或坐一二日，或三四日。其無理者，必獲證候而出，或身上生瘡癤，或咳嗽發熱之類。有理者略無纖事。以此剖判曲直，謂之天獄。蓋其土地之靈，有如此也。

白話文**(Vernacular)**：

又兩家爭訟，無法知道誰是誰非。王宮之對岸有小石塔十二座，令二人各坐一塔中。塔之外，兩家各派親屬互相提防。或坐一、二日，或三、四日。其無理者，必有徵候出現，或身上生瘡癤，或咳嗽發熱之類。有理者一點都無事。以此來判斷誰是誰非，謂之天獄。因為其土地有靈氣，所以可以這樣。

The second one is when there are disputes between two families, and it is unknown who is right or wrong. On the shore opposite the palace, there are twelve small stone towers; the arbitrator will ask both sides to sit in any one tower respectively. Outside the tower, members of the two families keep watch over one another. They may sit in the tower for one or two days or three or four days. If one is in the wrong, it must be that some symptoms will appear, for example, skin ulcer, cough, fever, etc. If one is in the right, then he will be fine. This method of judging right and wrong is called "judgment by God". That is the result of the land having a spiritual being.

15. 病癩
15. Illness and Leprosy

國人尋常有病，多是入水浸浴，及頻頻洗頭，便自痊可。然多病癩者，比比道途間。土人雖與之同臥同食亦不校。或謂彼中風土有此疾。又云曾有國主患此疾，故人不之嫌。以愚意觀之，往往好色之餘，便入水澡洗，故成此疾。聞土人色慾纔畢，皆入水澡洗。其患痢者十死八九。亦有貨藥於市者，與中國之藥不類，不知其為何物。更有一等師巫之屬，與人行持，尤為可笑。

白話文**(Vernacular)**：

國人通常有病，多是到水裡浸浴，及頻頻洗頭，便可自然痊癒。然生癩病的人很多，在路上可看到很多生癩病的人。土人雖與這些人同臥同食亦不計較。有的人說該地有此風土病。又說曾有國主患此疾病，所以人們不討厭此病。以我的觀察，往往在行房之後，便入水洗澡，故會生此病。聽說土人在行房後，馬上入水洗澡。其患痢疾者十有八、九人死。亦有藥物在市場上賣，與中國之藥不同，不知其為何物。更有一種巫師之類，為人治病，尤為可笑。

In this country, if people get sick, generally by soaking in the water and washing their heads several times, they can recover. We can see many people walking on the road who are infected with the illness of leprosy. The natives have not to care about sleeping and eating with them. They say that this is an endemic disease. Again they said once a Lord got this disease of leprosy, the people didn't avoid it. In my humble view, the people immediately go to bathe in the waters after making love, thus they are infected with this disease. I also heard that the natives, who immediately go to bathe in the waters after making love, get dysentery and die in eight or nine out of ten cases. They have drugs for sale in the market, but they are quite different from Chinese drugs. I do not know what the function of those drugs is. There is one man who is like a wizard in curing the disease; it is particularly ridiculous.

16. 死亡
16. Death

人死無棺，止貯以簟席之類，蓋之以布。其出喪也，前亦用旗幟鼓樂之屬。又以兩柈，盛以炒米，繞路拋撒，擡至城外僻遠無人之地，棄擲而去。俟有鷹鴉犬畜來食，頃刻而盡，則謂父母有福，故獲此報。若不食，或食而不盡，反謂父母有罪而至此。今亦漸有焚者，往往皆是唐人之遺種也。父母死，別無服制，男子則盡髠其髮，女子則於頂門翦髮如錢大，以此為孝耳。國主乃有塔葬埋，但不知葬身與葬骨耳。

白話文(Vernacular)：

人死不使用棺木，僅存放在竹席之上，上面蓋布。其出殯時，前導亦使用旗幟鼓樂之類。又以兩個盤子盛炒米，沿路拋撒，擡至城外僻遠無人之地，棄擲而去。等候老鷹、烏鴉、犬畜等來食，短時間內吃盡，就說父母有福，故才獲此福報。若不食，或食而不盡，反而說父母有罪才至此。今亦漸有使用焚化，往往皆是華人之後裔。父母死，並無服喪成規，男子則盡理光其頭髮，女子則於頂門翦髮如錢幣大小，以此為孝順。國主死則埋葬在塔內，但不知是葬肉身或葬骨骸。

When people die, there is no coffin. They put the corpse on a bamboo mat and cover it with cloth. There are flags and drumming music accompanying the funeral. They use two plates filled with fried rice and throw it along the road. The body is carried outside of the city to a remote and uninhabited place, and then is put down and left. The vultures, crows, and dogs come to eat the body. If the body is consumed quite soon, then they say their parents have a blessing, and so have received a reward. If the body is never eaten or eaten only partly, then they say that is because their parents committed a crime. Nowadays, cremation is increasingly executed; all of them always are the descendants of the Tángrén (the Chinese). When the parents die, there is no mourning regulation; the sons must shave all their head hair, and the daughters cut the hair on their forehead as big as a coin. This shows their filial piety for their parents. The Lord is buried in a tower, but I don't know if his body or bones are buried in the tower.

17. 耕種
17. Cultivation

大抵一歲中，可三四番收種。蓋四時常如五六月天，且不識霜雪故也。其地半年有雨，半年絕無。自四月至九月，每日下雨，午後方下。淡水洋中水痕高可七八丈，巨樹盡沒，僅留一杪耳。人家濱水而居者，皆移入山後。十月至三月，點雨絕無。洋中僅可通小舟，深處不過三五尺，人家又復移下，耕種者指至何時稻熟，是時水可淹至何處，隨其地而播種之。耕不用牛，耒耜鎌鋤之器，雖稍相類，而製自不同。然水傍又有一等野田，不種而常生稻，水高至一丈，而稻亦與之俱高，想別一種也。

白話文(Vernacular)：

　　大抵一年中，可收穫三、四次。蓋四時常如同五、六月天，且不識霜雪的緣故。其地半年有雨，半年絕無雨。自四月至九月，每日下雨，午後方下。淡水洋中水漲高可達七、八丈，巨樹盡沒入水中，僅留一樹梢。靠近水邊居住者，都搬到山後。十月至三月，一點雨都沒有。淡水洋中僅可通小舟，深處不過三、五尺，人們又遷移到水邊，耕種者知道至何時稻會成熟，何時水可淹至何處，隨其地而播種。耕田不用牛，它的耒、耜、鎌、鋤之器具，雖與中國的稍相類似，而製作方法不同。然水傍又有一種野田，不種而常生稻，水高至一丈，而稻亦與之長高，我想這是另一品種的稻子。

Generally, there are three or four times of rice harvests in a year, for the four seasons are the same as May or June of the Chinese calendar. Here is no frost and snow, and it rains for half a year and doesn't rain for half a year. From April to September, every day in the afternoon it rains. The waters of Tonle Sap Lake are over the watermark by seventy or eighty feet; all the huge trees are submerged in the waters, with only the treetops out of the water. The people who live around the lake move to the mountain areas. From October to March, there is no rain; only small boats can sail on the lake. The depth of the lake is but three to five feet. The people move once again to the shore. The cultivators know when the rice will be ripe and where the land will be flooded by the waters, and they sow the seeds with the change of the waters. They plow the land without using the cows. Their plow's handle, plow, sickle, and hoe are the same as China, but they are made in a different way. There is another uncultivated land, where the rice usually grows even without planting. When the waters flood reaching ten feet high, the rice grows at that height too. I think this is another kind of rice.

但畬田及種蔬,皆不用穢,嫌其不潔也。唐人到彼,皆不與之言及糞壅之事,恐為所鄙。每三兩家共掘地為一坑,蓋之以草;滿則填之。又別掘地為之。凡登溷既畢,必入池洗净。凡洗净止用左手,右手留以拿飯。見唐人登厠,用紙揩拭者皆笑之,甚至不欲其登門。婦女亦有立而溺者,可笑可笑。

白話文(Vernacular):

燒墾的田地及種蔬菜,皆不用糞便,嫌其不潔也。華人到該地,都不跟他們說糞便做肥料之事,恐為他們所鄙視。每三兩家共掘地為一坑,蓋之以草;滿則填之。又到別處掘地為之。凡是上完廁所,必入水池洗乾净。凡洗净只用左手,右手留以拿飯。見華人上廁所,用紙揩拭者皆笑之,甚至不讓他們登門。婦女亦有站立而尿者,可笑可笑。

They don't use manure to fertilize the fields and vegetables, thinking it is unclean. Tángrén (the Chinese) come here, without talking with them about the manure, for afraid of being despised. About three or four families dig jointly a hole for stooling, then covered it with straw. When this hole is filled up, they fill it with soil and dig another hole. Whenever they finish going to the toilet, they must go to wash themselves in a pond. They use only their left hand to wash and keep their right hand for taking food. The natives saw the Tángrén (the Chinese) going to the toilet, and cleaning themselves with paper and they laugh at them. Even the natives didn't want the Tángrén (the Chinese) in their housing. Some of the women also stand up to piss—it is so funny, so funny.

18. 山川
18. Mountains and Rivers

　　自入真蒲以來，率多平林叢木，長江巨港，綿亙數百里。古樹修藤，森陰蒙翳，禽獸之聲，雜遝於其間。至半港而始見有曠田，絕無寸木，彌望芃芃，禾黍而已。野牛以千百成羣，聚於其地。又有竹坡，亦綿亙數百里。其竹節間生刺，筍味至苦。四畔皆有高山。

　　白話文(Vernacular)：
　　自從我進入真蒲以來，所看到的大多是平林叢木，長江巨港，綿亙數百里。古樹長藤，森陰遮蔽，禽獸之聲，吵雜在其間。至半港而始見有空曠的田地，絕無一寸樹木，一眼望去，就是長得茂盛的禾黍而已。野牛以千百成羣，聚於其地。又有竹林長在山坡上，亦綿亙數百里。其竹節間生刺，筍味至苦。四周皆有高山。

Since coming to Zhen-pu, there are many equally high

trees and bushes, a long river, and a large port, which extends to several hundred li. The old trees and spreading rattan look thick and obscure. The animals make sounds among the trees. Arriving at Bàn-gǎng, the view becomes wide fields, completely no trees. When you gaze afar, there is nothing but fields of lush rice. Thousands of wild buffaloes gather here. There the bamboo grows on the slope, spreading over several hundred li. Those bamboos have thorns in their knots. The bamboo shoots have a very bitter taste. There are high mountains in all four directions.

19. 出產
19. Products

山多異木，無木處乃犀、象屯聚養育之地。珍禽奇獸，不計其數。細色有翠毛、象牙、犀角、黃蠟；粗色有降真、荳蔻、畫黃、紫梗、大風子油。

白話文(Vernacular)：

山多奇異的樹木，沒有樹木的地方就是犀、象屯聚養育之地。珍禽奇獸，不計其數。精細顏色的有翠毛、象牙、犀角、黃蠟；粗糙顏色的有降真、荳蔻、畫黃、紫梗、大風子油。

There are various kinds of trees in the mountains. Where there are no trees, rhinos, and elephants come together and rear their young. There are countless rare birds and strange beasts. Fine things include kingfisher feathers, ivory, rhino horns, and beeswax; coarse things include rosewood, cardamom, gamboge, lac, and chaulmoogra oil.

翡翠，其得也頗難。蓋叢林中有池，池中有魚，翡翠自林中飛出求魚，番人以樹葉蔽身，而坐水濱，籠一雌以誘之。手持小網，伺其來則罩之。有一日獲三五隻，有終日全不得者。

白話文(Vernacular)：

翡翠，要得到它頗難。蓋叢林中有水池，池中有魚，翡翠自林中飛出找魚吃，番人以樹葉遮蔽自己的身體，而坐在水邊，籠子裡關了一隻雌鳥以誘捕公鳥。手持小網，伺其飛來則罩之。一日可捕獲三、五隻，有時一整天都抓不到。

Kingfishers are really quite difficult to catch. Where there is a pond, the kingfishers fly out of the woods to catch the fish in the pond. The barbarians cover their body with leaves and sit by the side of the pond. They capture a female kingfisher in a cage as bait to seduce a male one. They wait for the males to come, then put a small net over them. Sometimes they can catch three to five birds in a day; sometimes they catch nothing all day.

象牙則山僻人家有之。每一象死，方有二牙，舊傳謂每歲一換牙者，非也。其牙以標而殺之者為上也，自死而隨時為人所取者次之，死於山中多年者，斯為下矣。

白話文(Vernacular)：

象牙則山中偏僻人家才有。每一隻象死了，有二隻象牙，舊傳謂每年換一次牙，並非如此。其牙以射標而殺之者為上等，自然死亡而隨時為人所取得者次之，死於山中多年者，則為下等。

The ivory comes from the people who live in the remote mountain areas. For every elephant that dies, there are only two tusks of ivory. The old saying that elephants change their ivory each year is incorrect. An elephant killed by a lance would produce the best ivory. The ivory of elephants dying a natural death and collected at any time by the people would be the next quality. The ivory of elephants that have been dead for many years in the mountains would be bad in quality.

黃蠟出於村落朽樹間，其一種細腰蜂如螻蟻者，番人取而得之，每一船可收二、三千塊，每塊大者三、四十斤，小者亦不下十八九斤。

白話文(Vernacular)：

黃蠟（蜂蜜）出於村落朽樹上，由一種細腰蜂如螻蟻者所製造的蜂蜜，番人取得它，每一船可收二、三千塊，每塊大者三、四十斤，小者亦不下十八、九斤。

The barbarians get beeswax which is produced by a kind of bee with a narrow waist like an ant. That bee lives in rotten trees in the villages. Every boat can load two to three thousand lumps of beeswax. A large lump amounts to thirty or forty pounds, and a small one is not less than eighteen to nineteen pounds.

犀角白而帶花者為上，黑而無花者為下。

白話文(Vernacular)：

犀角白而帶花者為上等，黑而無花者為下等。

Rhino horn with white color and veining is the best quality; black color without veining is the lower quality.

降真生叢林中，番人頗費砍斫之勞，蓋此乃樹之心耳。其外白，木可厚八九寸，小者亦不下四五寸。

白話文(Vernacular)：

降真生叢林中，番人頗費砍斫之辛勞，蓋此乃樹心。其外白色，木可厚八、九寸，小者亦不下四、五寸。

Rosewood grows in the jungle. The barbarians must spend a lot of effort cutting and chopping down the trees. Rosewood grows really in the central part of the trees. Rosewood's skin is white in color, and its trunk is about eight to nine inches thick. Even a small one is no less than four or five inches.

荳蔻皆野人山上所種。畫黃乃一等樹間之脂；番人預先一年以刀斫樹，滴瀝其脂，至次年而始收。

白話文(Vernacular)：

荳蔻皆野人山上所種。畫黃乃一種樹流出之脂；番人預先一年以刀砍樹，讓其脂滴漏下來，至次年始採收。

The cardamoms are cultivated by the barbarians in the mountains. The gamboge is the resin from a kind of tree. The barbarians must cut the tree one year in advance, so its resin falls slowly down in drops until the next year's harvest.

紫梗生於一等樹枝間，正如桑寄生之狀，亦頗難得。

白話文**(Vernacular)**：

紫梗生於一種樹枝間，正如桑樹寄生之情況，亦頗難得。

The lac grows on the branches of a kind of tree, it looks like mulberry parasitism, and also it is not easy to obtain.

大風子油乃大樹之子，狀如椰子而圓，中有子數十枚。

白話文**(Vernacular)**：

大風子油乃大樹之種籽，形狀如椰子而圓，中有籽數十粒。

The chaulmoogra oil comes from the seeds of a large tree. Its fruit shape looks as round as a coconut, and there are over ten seeds within it.

胡椒間亦有之，纏藤而生，纍纍如綠草子，其生而青者更辣。

白話文**(Vernacular)**：

當中亦有胡椒，纏藤而生，纍纍如綠草子，它還沒熟而青者更辣。

There are also peppers that grow and climb up on the rattan and fructify like seeds of grass. When they are not yet mature and with green color, they are still hotter yet.

20. 貿易
20. Trade

國人交易皆婦人能之，所以唐人到彼，必先納一婦者，兼亦利其能買賣故也。

白話文(Vernacular)：

國人交易皆婦人在做，所以華人到該地，必先納一婦女，兼亦得利於其能做買賣之緣故。

The local people who engage in business are all women. Thus, when Tángrén (the Chinese) comes here, the first thing is to marry a local woman in order to get the benefit of her business capability.

每日一墟，自卯至午即罷。無鋪店，但以蓬席之類鋪於地間，各有常處，聞亦有納官司賃地錢。小交關則用米穀及唐貨，次則用布；若乃大交關，則用金銀矣。

白話文(Vernacular)：

每日一市場，自早上五點至中午一點即結束。無鋪店，都以草席之類鋪於地上，每人都有經常擺攤的地點，聽說也有繳納給官方的租地錢。小交易，使用米穀及中國貨品，次則用布；若有大筆交易，則使用金和銀。

The market is open every day from five o'clock in the morning to one o'clock in the afternoon. There are no stores, but everything is laid out on straw mats on the ground. Their stalls always stay in the same place. I heard that they also pay the officials to rent the place. As to a small transaction, they pay with rice and Chinese goods; for a bigger transaction, they pay with cloth; for a larger transaction, they pay with gold and silver.

往年土人最朴，見唐人頗加敬畏，呼之為佛，見則伏地頂禮。近亦有脫騙欺負唐人者矣，由去人之多故也。

白話文(Vernacular)：

往年土人最樸實，見到華人頗加敬畏，稱他為佛，見面則伏地頂禮。近來則也有欺騙欺負華人，此乃前往該地的華人人數多了的緣故。

In the past years, the natives are very polite and simple, and when they meet the Tángrén (the Chinese), they always express respect and awe. They call the Tángrén (the Chinese) as a Buddha and prostrate on the ground and kowtow when they see the Tángrén (the Chinese). However, recently they sometimes cheat and bully the Tángrén (the Chinese), for many Tángrén (the Chinese) come to this country.

21. 欲得唐貨
21. Desire for Tang Goods

其地想不出金銀，以唐人金銀為第一，五色輕縑帛次之；其次如真州之錫鑞、溫州之漆盤、泉處之青甆器，及水銀、銀硃、紙箚、硫黃、焰硝、檀香、草芎、白芷、麝香、麻布、黃草布、雨傘、鐵鍋、銅盤、水硃、桐油、篦箕、木梳、針。其粗重則如明州之蓆。甚欲得者，則菽麥也，然不可將去耳。

白話文(Vernacular)：

其地不出產金和銀，以華人金和銀為第一，五色輕薄絲織品次之；其次如真州之錫和鉛錫合金、溫州之漆盤、泉州之青甆器，及水銀、銀硃、紙箚、硫黃、焰硝、檀香、草芎、白芷、麝香、麻布、黃草布、雨傘、鐵鍋、銅盤、水硃、桐油、篦箕、木梳和針等。其粗重則如明州之草蓆。甚欲得者，是豆子和麥子，然不可從中國輸出到該國。

This country does not produce gold and silver, so they need first the Tángrén (Chinese) gold and silver; the next is five colors of fine light silk; the next after that are, such things as Zhen-chou's tin-lead wares, Wen-chou's lacquer plates, Quan-chou's green porcelain, and mercury, silver cinnabar, paper, sulfur, flame, sandalwood, lovage, angelica dahurica, musk, burlap, yellow grass cloth, umbrellas, iron pots, copper plates, water cinnabar, tung tree oil, bamboo scoops, wooden combs, needles. They also need mats the size and as heavy as Ming-chou's. Beans and wheat are desired products, but they can't be exported from China to there.

22. 草木
22. Flora

惟石榴、甘蔗、荷花、蓮藕、羊桃、蕉芎與中國同。荔枝、橘子狀雖同而味酸，其餘皆中國所未曾見。樹木亦甚各別。草花更多，且香而艷。水中之花，更有多品，皆不知其名。至若桃、李、杏、梅、松、柏、杉、檜、梨、棗、楊、柳、桂、蘭、菊、芷之類，皆所無也。正月亦有荷花。

白話文(Vernacular)：
惟石榴、甘蔗、荷花、蓮藕、羊桃、蕉芎與中國同。荔枝、橘子之形狀雖同而味酸，其餘皆中國所未曾見。樹木亦甚為不同。草花更多，且香而艷。水中之花，更有多品，皆不知其名。至若桃、李、杏、梅、松、柏、杉、檜、梨、棗、楊、柳、桂、蘭、菊、芷之類，該地都沒有。正月亦有荷花。

This country produces pomegranate, sugar cane, lotus, lotus root, carambola, and banana, all of which are the same as China. Although the shape of lychees and oranges is similar to China, their taste is so sour. The rest we have never seen in China. The trees are also quite different from China. There have more grasses and flowers, which are very fragrant and beautiful. The flowers growing in the waters have variant categories, and I do not know their names. As to peach, plum (li), apricot, plum (mei), pine, cypress, cedar, juniper, pear, jujube, poplar, willow, laurel, orchid, chrysanthemum, angelica, they do not have any of them. They have also lotus flowers in January.

23. 飛鳥
23. Flying Birds

禽有孔雀、翡翠、鸚鵡，乃中國所無。其餘如鷹、鴉、鷺鶯、雀兒、鸕鷀、鸛、鶴、野鴨、黃雀等物皆有之。所無者，喜鵲、鴻雁、黃鶯、杜宇、燕、鴿之屬。

白話文(Vernacular)：
禽類有孔雀、翡翠、鸚鵡，乃中國所無。其餘如鷹、鴉、鷺鶯、雀兒、鸕鷀、鸛、鶴、野鴨、黃雀等物皆有。所沒有的是喜鵲、鴻雁、黃鶯、杜宇、燕、鴿之類。

As to birds, they have peacocks, kingfishers, and parrots,

of which China has none. Otherwise, they have the following birds, such as eagle, crow, egret, sparrow, cormorant, stork, crane, wild duck, siskin, etc. But they don't have magpies, wild geese, oriole, cuckoo, swallow and pigeon.

24. 走獸
24. Animals

　　獸有犀、象、野牛、山馬，乃中國所無者。其餘如虎、豹、熊、羆、野豬、麋鹿、麞、麂、猿、狐之類甚多。所不見者，獅子、猩猩、駱駝耳。雞、鴨、牛、馬、豬、羊在所不論也。馬甚矮小，牛甚多，生不敢騎，死不敢食，亦不敢剝其皮，聽其腐爛而已。以其與人出力故也，但以駕車耳。在先無鵝，近有舟人自中國攜去，故得其種。鼠有大如貓者；又有一等鼠，頭腦絕類新生小狗兒。

　　白話文**(Vernacular)**：
　　獸類有犀、象、野牛、山馬，乃中國所無者。其餘如虎、豹、熊、羆、野豬、麋鹿、麞、麂、猿、狐之類甚多。在這裡沒有看到獅子、猩猩、駱駝。雞、鴨、牛、馬、豬、羊在這裡是有的。馬甚矮小，牛甚多，一般人不敢騎，不敢食死牛，亦不敢剝其皮，讓其腐爛而已。由於牛為人出力之緣故，只用來駕車。起先這裡沒有鵝，近有船人自中國帶去，故得傳種繁衍。老鼠有大如貓者；又有一種鼠，頭腦類似新生小狗兒。

They have animals, such as rhinoceros, elephants, bison, and mountain horse, of which China has none. Otherwise, they have tigers, leopards, bears, brown bears, wild boars, elks, roe deer, muntjak, apes, foxes, etc. But they have no lion, orangutan, or camel. Of course, they have chicken, duck, cow, horse, pig, and goat. Here the horse is small and short. There are a great many cows. The local people dare not ride on a cow when the cow is alive, not eat them when they die, or peel its skin. They just leave the cow to rot away. This is because the cow exerts great effort to haul the carts for human beings. Originally, there were no geese, but recently sailors brought them from China to this country. So they can be raised and propagated forever. There have rats as large as cats. There is also a kind of mouse whose head looks just like a newborn puppy's.

25. 蔬菜
25. Vegetables

蔬菜有蔥、芥、韭、茄、西瓜、冬瓜、王瓜、莧菜。所無者蘿蔔、生菜、苦蕒、菠薐之類。瓜、茄正二月間即有之。茄樹有經數年不除者。木綿花樹高可過屋，有十餘年不換者。不識名之菜甚多，水中之菜亦多種。

白話文**(Vernacular)**：

蔬菜有蔥、芥、韭、茄、西瓜、冬瓜、王瓜、莧菜。所無者蘿蔔、生菜、苦蕒、菠薐之類。瓜、茄正二月間即有之。茄樹有經數年不砍除者。木綿花樹高可超過屋頂，有十餘年不換種其他樹。不識名之菜甚多，水中之菜亦多種。

They have the following vegetables, such as onion,

mustard, chive, eggplant, watermelon, winter gourd, king snake gourd, and amaranth. But they have no radish, lettuce, bitter chicory, or spinach. The production of melons and eggplants is available in February. They do not uproot the eggplants for over ten years. They grow the kapok trees for over ten years and their height is taller than the roof of a house. But they didn't change it to plant other trees. There are many vegetables whose names I do not know. Many vegetables are planted in the water.

26. 魚龍
26. Fish and Reptiles

魚鱉惟黑鯉魚最多，其他如鯉、鯽、草魚亦多。有吐哺魚，大者重二斤以上。更有不識名之魚亦甚多，此皆淡水洋中所來者。至若海中之魚，色色有之。鱔魚、湖鰻，田雞土人不食，入夜則縱橫道途間。黿鼉大如合柱，雖六藏[22]之龜，亦充食用。查南之蝦，重一斤以上。真蒲龜腳可長八九寸許。鱷魚大者如船，有四腳，絕類龍，特無角耳，肚甚脆美。蛤、蜆、螺螄之屬，淡水洋中可捧而得。獨不見蟹，想亦有之，而人不食耳。

白話文(Vernacular)：

魚鱉惟黑鯉魚最多，其他如鯉、鯽、草魚亦多。有吐哺魚，大者重二斤以上。更有不知名之魚亦甚多，此皆淡

---

[22] 六藏之龜，指將頭、尾和四足等六體縮藏在龜殼內的烏龜。

The six-hide tortoise refers to a tortoise that hides its six bodies, including the head, tail and four feet, in the tortoise shell.

水洋中所產者。至若海中之魚，各種都有。鱔魚、湖鰻，田雞土人不食，入夜則縱橫道路間。黿鼉大如合抱的柱子，雖六藏之龜，亦充食用。查南之蝦，重一斤以上。真蒲龜腳可長八、九寸許。鱷魚大者像船一樣，有四腳，非常類似龍，只是沒有角，肚子甚是脆美。蛤、蜆、螺螄之類，淡水洋中可捧而得。獨不見蟹，我想應該有，但當地人不吃。

There is a lot of fish, turtle, black carp, and also carp, Gi carp, and grass carp. There are Tu-Fu fish of which a large one can weigh over two pounds. There are also a lot of nameless fish which are coming from the Tonle Sap Lake. As to the sea fish, there are also various kinds. The natives don't eat the eel, lake eel, and frog, which climb in the road at night. There are giant turtles as big as pillars. The natives eat the turtles. Shrimps in Cha-nan weigh over one pound. In Zhen-pu, a turtle's feet can be eight or nine inches long. Crocodiles are as big as a boat. They have four feet and look exactly like a dragon, but no horns. The abdomen of a crocodile tastes good and crisp. There are clams, small clams, and river snails all of which can be fished from the Tonle Sap Lake. There is probably a crab, but I didn't see any. However, the natives do not eat them.

27. 醞釀
27. Brewing

酒有四等：第一等唐人呼為蜜糖酒，用藥麴，以蜜及水中半為之。其次者，土人呼為朋牙四，以樹葉為之。朋牙四者，乃一等樹葉之名也。又其次，以米或以剩飯為之，名曰包稜角。蓋包稜角者米也。其下有糖鑑酒，以糖為之。又入港濱水，人家有茭漿酒；蓋有一等茭葉生於水濱，其漿可以釀酒。

白話文**(Vernacular)**：

酒有四種：第一種華人稱為蜜糖酒，用藥麴，以蜜及水對半調和製成。其次者，土人稱為朋牙四，以樹葉製成。朋牙四者，乃一種樹葉之名也。又其次，以米或以剩飯製成，名曰包稜角。蓋包稜角者米也。其下有糖鑑酒，以糖製成。又入港水邊人家有茭漿酒；蓋有一種茭葉生於水濱，其漿可以釀酒。

There have four kinds of wine. The first is what the Tángrén (Chinese) call "Honey-sugar wine", which is made by mixing medicinal yeast with honey and water. The second is what the natives call "Pen-ya-si", which is made from the leaves of some kind of tree. The so-called "Pen-ya-si" is the name of the leaf. The third is called "Bao-len-jiao", which is made of rice or leftovers. The so-called "Bao-len-jiao" is rice. The fourth is called "Sugar-Jien wine", which is made from sugar. Furthermore, there are the people living on the waterfront of the port, who have water bamboo shoots pulp wine. The water bamboo shoots grow along the waterfront and are mashed into a pulp to make wine.

28. 鹽醋醬麴

28. Salt, Vinegar, Sauce and Yeast

醃物國中無禁，自真蒲、巴澗濱海等處，率皆燒滷為之。山間更有一等石，味勝於鹽，可琢以成器。

白話文(Vernacular)：

製鹽物該國沒有禁止，自真蒲、巴澗濱海等處，都有燒鹹水製鹽。山間更有一種石頭，味勝於鹽，可雕琢成器具。

There is no prohibition on salt-making in this country. From the seafront of Zhen-pu to Ba-jien the people cook seawater to make salt. In the mountains, there is a kind of rock that tastes better than salt, and even can be cut and polished into utensils.

土人不能為醋，羹中欲酸，則著以咸平樹葉，樹既生莢則用莢，既生子則用子。

白話文(Vernacular)：

土人不會製醋，羹中欲酸，則放入咸平樹葉，樹若生莢則用莢，若生子則用子。

The natives can't make vinegar. If they want the soup to taste sour, they add a leaf of the "Sianping (tamarind)" tree. If the tree has pods, they use the pods. If the tree has the seeds, they use the seeds.

亦不識合醬，為無麥與豆故也。亦不曾造麴，蓋以蜜水及樹葉釀酒，所用者酒藥耳，亦如鄉間白酒藥之狀。

白話文(Vernacular)：

亦不識醬油，因為沒有麥與豆的緣故。亦不曾造麴，因為以蜜水及樹葉釀酒，所用的是酵母，亦如鄉間白酵母之形狀。

The natives also don't know how to make soy sauce, because they don't raise wheat and beans. They can't make yeast, so make wine from honey, water, and leaves. They use wine yeast which is similar to white wine yeast in our countryside.

29. 蠶桑
29. Silk Production

土人皆不事蠶桑，婦人亦不曉針線縫補之事，僅能織木綿布而已。亦不能紡，但以手捏成條。無機杼以織，但以一頭縛腰，一頭搭窗上。梭亦止用一竹管。

白話文(Vernacular)：

土人皆不事蠶桑，婦人亦不曉得針線縫補之事，僅能織木綿布而已。亦不能紡織，僅能以手捏成條。無機杼織成布料，以一頭縛在腰間，一頭搭在窗上。梭亦僅用一竹管。

The natives don't raise silkworms nor plant mulberry; women also don't know needle and thread sewing. They can only weave the cloth of kapok. They don't know spinning but rub their hands to make cotton into a thread. There is no loom for weaving. They tie one end of the thread to their waist, and another end to a window, and use a bamboo tube as a shuttle.

近年暹人來居，卻以蠶桑為業。桑種蠶種，皆自暹中來。亦無麻苧,惟有絡麻。暹人卻以絲自織皂綾衣著,暹婦卻能縫補。土人打布損破,皆倩其補之。

白話文(Vernacular):

近年暹人來居此國,有以蠶桑為業。桑種蠶種,皆自暹國運來。亦無麻苧,惟有絡麻。暹人以絲自織皂綾衣服,暹婦卻能縫補。土人之打布損破,皆請暹婦縫補。

In recent years, Sien people come to live here, and they earn their living with silk production. The breed of mulberry and silkworm comes from Sien country. There is no ramie, but they have hemp. Sien people weave black damask garments with silk, and Sien women know how to sew and make up clothes. When the natives wear and attrite their clothes, they always ask them to patch their clothes up.

30. 器用
30. Utensils

尋常人家,房舍之外,別無桌凳盂桶之類,但作飯則用一瓦釜,作羹則用一瓦銚。就地埋三石為竈。以椰子殼為杓。盛飯用中國瓦盤或銅盤;羹則用樹葉造一小碗,雖盛汁亦不漏。又以茭葉製一小杓,用兜汁入口,用畢則棄之。雖祭祀神佛亦然。又以一錫器或瓦器盛水於傍,用以蘸手。蓋飯只用手拿,其粘於手者,非水不能去也。

白話文(Vernacular):

一般人家,房舍之外,別無桌子、凳子、盂桶之類,但作飯則用一瓦釜,作羹則用一瓦瓶。就地埋三石為竈。以椰子殼為杓子。盛飯用中國瓦盤或銅盤;羹則用樹葉造一小碗，雖盛汁亦不漏。又以茭葦葉製一小杓，用來舀湯汁入口，用完就丟棄。祭祀神佛也是使用同樣的容器。又以一錫器或瓦器盛水於傍，用手去沾水。因為只用手拿飯，會粘在手上，沾水就不會黏在手上。

The ordinary people have housing, but no tables, chairs, and basins. They use clay pots to cook rice and clay bottles to cook soup and put them on a stove of three stones. They use a coconut shell as a dipper. They put rice on a Chinese ceramic plate or copper plate. They use the leaves to make up a small bowl for holding soup without leaking. They make a small dipper from the Kajang leaves, which are used for drinking soup, and thrown away after using it. The same container is used for offering sacrifices to gods and Buddhas. On the side there is water loaded in a tin or tile pot; it is for dipping their hand in. Since you use your right hand to take rice which will stick to your hand. It won't stick to your hands when your hand gets wet.

飲酒則用鑞器，可盛三四盞許，其名為蛤；盛酒則用鑞注子。貧人則用瓦缽子。若府第富室，則一一用銀，至有用金者。國主處多用金器，制度形狀又別。

白話文(**Vernacular**)：

飲酒則用錫鉛容器，可盛三、四杯許，其名為蛤；盛酒則用錫鉛酒壺。貧人則用瓦缽子。若府第富室，則一一用銀器，至有用金器者。國主處多使用金器，制度和形狀又有不同。

They use a tin-lead container to drink wine, which can

contain three or four cups of wine, and the cup is called "kaew". They use a tin-lead pot to contain wine. The poor people use a clay pot. The big houses use all silver utensils. The Lord uses golden utensils of which the shape and quality are different and special.

地下所鋪者，明州之草蓆，或有鋪虎豹麂鹿等皮及藤簟者。近新置矮桌，高尺許。睡只竹蓆，臥於板。近又用矮床者，往往皆唐人製作也。食品用布罩。

白話文(Vernacular)：

地面所鋪設者，有明州之草蓆，或有鋪虎、豹、麂、鹿等皮及藤蓆。近新購置的矮桌，高一尺許。人們睡在木板上，它上面鋪竹蓆。近又使用矮床，往往都是華人製作的。食品用布罩罩起來。

They lay out Ming-chou grass mat on the ground. Some of the people lay out the fur of tiger, panther, muntjak, deer, or rattan mat. Recently, some people buy new low tables, one foot high. They sleep on a plank on which is laid a bamboo mat. Recently, they use a low bed which is usually made by the Tángrén (the Chinese). They use a cloth cover to mantle the food.

夜多蚊子，亦用布罩。國主內中，以銷金縑帛為之，皆舶商所饋也。

白話文(Vernacular)：

夜晚多蚊子，亦用布罩。國主宮中，以鑲金邊的絲織品製作蚊帳，都是外國船商所饋贈。

There are many mosquitoes in the evening, so they also use a cloth tent to protect against them. In the palace of the Lord, there use a tent of fine silk with golden lace which was contributed by big foreign ship merchants.

稻子不用礱磨，止用杵臼耳。

白話文(**Vernacular**)：

稻子不用礱磨稻穀去殼，僅用杵臼。

They don't use millstones to remove the husk of rice, but pestle and mortar.

31. 車轎
31. Carts and Palanquins

轎之制，以一木屈其中，兩頭竪起，雕刻花樣，以金銀裹之，所謂金銀轎槓者此也。每頭三尺之內釘一鉤子，以大布一條厚摺，用繩繫於兩頭鉤中，人坐於布內，以兩人擡之。轎外又加一物，如船篷而更闊，飾以五色縑帛，四人扛之，隨轎而走。

白話文(**Vernacular**)：

轎之結構，是以一木槓置入其中，兩頭竪起，雕刻花樣，外包裹以金銀，所謂金銀轎槓者就是這種。每頭三尺之內釘一鉤子，以大布一條厚摺，用繩繫於兩頭鉤中，人坐在布內，以兩人擡之。轎外又加一物，如船篷而更寬闊，裝飾以五色絲織品，有四人扛，隨轎而走。

The structure of a palanquin is to use a piece of wood as a carrying pole, both its ends upward and carved with flora designs and covered with gold and silver. This is what I meant by palanquin with gold and silver carrying pole. They nailed separately two hooks at a distance of three feet from both ends of the carrying pole. There is a rope to tie a large cloth to two hooks, then a person sits inside the cloth, and two persons lift it up at each end. In addition to the palanquin, there add one thing which is like a canopy of a boat, but much broader. It is decorated in fine five-colored silk. This container is raised by four persons and follows the palanquin.

圖 11：吳哥寺浮雕上的抬轎槓子

Figure 11: Palanquin

Sources: "Angkor Thom, Angkor Wat & Siem Reap (Cambodia)",

https://www.youtube.com/watch?v=CerAwJ4YnT8

圖 12：轎槓子上的掛勾

Figure 12: Palanquin hook

Sources:

https://www.pinterest.com/pin/618682067539202143/

圖 13：吳哥寺浮雕上的兩人抬轎子

Figure 13: Palanquin lifted by two men

Sources: "Angkor Thom - Cambodia.mov,"

https://www.youtube.com/watch?v=gkXMpxDuxmw

　　若遠行，亦有騎象、騎馬者，亦有用車者。車之制，卻與他地一般。馬無鞍，象卻有凳可坐。

　　白話文(Vernacular)：

　　若遠行，亦有騎象、騎馬的，亦有坐車的。車之型態，與他地一樣。馬無鞍，象卻有椅凳可坐。

    If they go far away, they ride on an elephant or horse or take carts. The style of the carts is similar to other places. But riding the horse, they don't use a saddle. There is a small stool on the back of an elephant, which one can sit on.

圖 **14**：吳哥寺浮雕上的馬車

Figure 14 : Horse Cart

Sources:

https://www.youtube.com/watch?v=96Aiy0D0VmA

圖 **15**：吳哥寺浮雕上的象的坐騎

Figure 15 : Stool on the back of Elephant

Sources:

https://www.youtube.com/watch?v=pCMAGofUKSw

32. 舟楫
32. Boats

巨舟以硬樹破板為之。匠者無鋸，但以斧鑿之，開成板；既費木，且費工，甚拙也。凡要木成段，亦只以鑿鑿斷；起屋亦然。船亦用鐵釘，上以茭葉蓋覆之，卻以檳榔木破片壓之。此船名為新拿，用櫂。所粘之油，魚油也；所和之灰，石灰也。

白話文(Vernacular)：

巨舟是以硬樹砍成木板製造而成。工匠沒有鋸子，而是以斧頭鑿之，劈開成木板；不僅浪費木，也浪費工，甚為笨拙。凡是木頭要砍成兩段，亦只有使用鑿刀鑿斷；造屋也是一樣。船亦用鐵釘，上以茭葉覆蓋，再以檳榔木破片壓之。此船名為新拿，用槳。船上所粘之油，是魚油；所和之灰，是石灰。

A large boat is made of planks of a hard log. The artisans have no saws but use an ax to cut the log into a plank. It wastes the wood and also their efforts, and is quite stupid. If they want several lengths of a log, the only way is to cut it off. To build a house is the same. To build a boat, they also use iron nails. They cover the boat with the leaves of water bamboo shoots and put areca wood to press on it. They use paddles for the boat, which they call "Xīn-ná". They use fish oil to stick the boat planks together and use lime to mortar the boat.

小舟卻以一巨木鑿成槽，以火薰軟，用木撐開；腹大，兩頭尖，無篷，可載數人；止以櫂劃之，名為皮蘭。

白話文(Vernacular)：

小舟則是以一巨木鑿空成槽狀，以火燻軟，用木撐開；中間腹部大，兩頭尖，無篷，可載數人；只以槳划之，名為皮蘭。

A small boat is made from a giant log cut into a trough shape, with a fire to smoke and make it pliable, then a log is used to open it up. The belly of a small boat is big, both ends are pointed; it has no canopy and can hold several people. Paddles are used to row it. Its name is "Pi-lan".

33. 屬郡

33. Local County

屬郡九十餘，曰真蒲，曰查南，曰巴澗，曰莫良，曰八薛，曰蒲買，曰雉棍，曰木津波，曰賴敢坑，曰八廝里。其餘不能悉記。各置官屬，皆以木排柵為城。

白話文(Vernacular)：

屬郡共有九十餘個，叫真蒲，叫查南，叫巴澗，叫莫良，叫八薛，叫蒲買，叫雉棍，叫木津波，叫賴敢坑，叫八廝里。其餘不能完全記得。各郡置官屬，皆以木排柵築城。

The number of local counties is over ninety, including Zhen-pu, Ba-jien, Mo-lian, Ba-xue, Pu-mai, Zhi-gun, Mu-jinpo, Lai-gan-keng, Ba-si-li. I can't remember the others. Every county sets up an office. The county is surrounded by a wooden grid and becomes a stockade.

34. 村落
34. Villages

　　每一村，或有寺，或有塔。人家稍密，亦自有鎮守之官，名為買節。大路上自有歇腳去處，如郵亭之類，其名為森木。近與暹人交兵，遂皆成曠地。
　　白話文(Vernacular)：
　　每一村，或有寺，或有塔。人口稍密，亦自行設有鎮守之官員，名為買節。大路上設有歇腳之處所，如郵亭之類，其名為森木。近與暹人交戰，遂皆成荒地。

In every village, there is a temple or pagoda. Where the population is more dense, an official called "Mai-jie" is set up and is responsible for the security of the village. There are rest places along the road, such as post-houses, called "Sen-mu". Recently, they have engaged in wars with the Sien people, which have resulted in wastelands.

35. 取膽
35. Taking Out Gall

　　前此於八月內取膽，蓋占城主每年索人膽一甕，可千餘枚。遇夜則多方令人於城中及村落去處。遇有夜行者，以繩兜住其頭，用小刀於右脅下取去其膽，俟數足，以饋占城主。獨不取唐人之膽，蓋因一年取唐人一膽雜於其中，遂致甕中之膽俱臭腐而不可用故也。近年已除取膽之事，另置取膽官屬，居北門之裏。

白話文(**Vernacular**)：

前次是在八月內取膽，蓋占城主每年索人膽一甕，數量達千餘枚。遇夜則多方派人於城中及村落去處。遇有夜行者，以繩兜住其頭，用小刀於其右脅下挖取其膽，等待數量夠了，饋贈給占城主。唯有不取華人之膽，因為有一年取華人一膽雜於其它的膽中，遂致甕中之膽全部臭腐而不可用的緣故。近年已廢除取膽之事，另設置取膽官屬，位居北門之裏面。

Previously, they took out human gall[23] in August, to respond to the Lord of Champa's demand of one urn of over one thousand galls every year. At night, they order someone to go to towns and villages. When they meet a person walking in the night, they set a rope around his neck. They dig out his gall with a knife from his lower right chest. When the numbers of gall are enough, they give it to the Lord of Champa. They don't take the gall of the Chinese people, because once a year they took a Chinese gall and mixed it with the other men's gall resulting then in the whole urn of gall being corrupted and unusable. Recently, gall-taking has been abolished. They established a gall-taking official who resided inside the north

---

[23] 取人膽的目的有二，一是用來洗大象的眼睛，二是表示占城人勇敢及預防疾病。

The purpose of taking human gall is to wash the eyes of elephants, or the people of Champa eat the gall to strengthen their courage and avoid disease.

gate of the city.

36. 異事
36. Strange Things

東門之裏，有蠻人淫其妹者，皮肉相粘不開，歷三日不食而俱死。余鄉人薛氏，居番三十五年矣，渠謂兩見此事。蓋其用聖佛之靈，所以如此。

白話文(Vernacular)：

東門之裏面，有蠻人淫其妹者，皮肉相粘不能脫開，歷三日不食而兩人都死。我的鄉人薛氏，住在這裡三十五年，他說見過該種事兩次。因為他擁有聖佛之靈氣，所以能看到此事。

Inside the east gate, there is a barbarian who had sex with his young sister. The skin and flesh of both people stuck together and could not be separated. After three days, both people died of starvation. My fellow countryman Mr. Xue, who has lived in Zhen-la for thirty-five years, said he saw such a thing twice. Because he has the spiritual power of holy Buddha, he can do that.

37. 澡浴
37. Bathing

地苦炎熱，每日非數次澡洗則不可過，入夜亦不免一二次。初無浴室盂桶之類，但每家須有一池；否則亦兩三家合一池。不分男女，皆裸體入池。惟父母尊年者在池，則子女卑幼不敢入。或卑幼先在池，則尊年者亦廻避之。如行（女）輩，則無拘也，但以左手遮其牝門入水而已。

白話文(Vernacular)：

該地最苦的是天氣炎熱，每日需洗澡數次，否則不舒服，入夜亦不免洗浴一、二次。初無浴室盂桶之類，但每家須有一水池；否則亦兩三家合建一水池。不分男女，皆裸體入池。惟父母年長者在池，則子女卑幼不敢入內。或卑幼先在池，則年長者亦廻避。如果是女輩入池，則無所拘束，她們只以左手遮其私處入水而已。

This country is very hot, and one must bathe several times a day, otherwise, it is hard to endure. In the evening the people need to go bathing once or twice. They have no bathing rooms or bathing tubs but prepare a pond. Otherwise, two or three families unite to use a pond. No matter whether men or women, all are naked in the pond. When the parents and seniors have already been in the pond, then the children and juniors dare not go into the pond. If the juniors had already been in a pond in advance, then the seniors avoid entering the pond. If they are women, there is no restraint for them; they just use their left hand to cover their pussy.

或三四日，或五六日，城中婦女三三五五咸至城外河中澡洗，至河邊脫去所纏之布而入水。會聚於河者，動以千數，雖府第婦女亦預焉，略不以為恥。自踵至頂，皆得而見之。城外大河，無日無之。唐人暇日頗以此為遊觀之樂。聞亦有就水中偷期者。水常溫如湯，惟五更則微涼，至日出則復溫矣。

白話文(**Vernacular**)：

或三、四日，或五、六日，城中婦女三三五五都到城外河中洗澡，至河邊脫去所纏之布而入水。會聚於河的人數，有時達千人，雖府第婦女亦有參加，她們並不以此為羞恥。自腳到頭頂，都可以看得見。城外大河，沒有一天沒有人洗澡。華人在假日頗以此為遊觀之樂。聽說亦有人潛入水中偷看。水常溫如湯，惟到了清晨三點到五點則微涼，至日出則恢復溫熱。

About three or four days, or five or six days, the women in the city get together in several groups going out of the city. They go bathing in the river. They take off their clothes and enter into the water. Several thousand women, including the women of the big houses, jointly go bathing in the river. They don't feel it is shameful. Their whole body from head to foot can be seen by other people. Every day there are many women going out of the city for bathing in the big river. On their leisure days, the Tángrén (Chinese) feel it is a pleasure to watch those women bathing. I heard that some of them like to peep under the water. The water of the river is always warm as a hot soup. It will only be a little cooler in the fifth watch (about 3:00 to 5:00 am). It increasingly warms up again at sunrise.

38. 流寓

38. Emigrant

唐人之為水手者，利其國中不著衣裳，且米糧易求，婦女易得，屋室易辦，器用易足，買賣易為，往往皆逃逸於彼。

白話文**(Vernacular)**：

華人擔任水手者，對其有利的是該國不穿衣裳，且米糧易求得，婦女易獲得，屋室易購辦，器用易滿足，買賣易進行，所以都逃至該國。

The sailors of the Tángrén (Chinese) live in this country, due to wearing no more clothes, rice, and food are easy to earn, women are easy to get, housing is easy to deal with, utensils are easy to use, and it is easy to do business. Therefore, they always run away from China to be here.

39. 軍馬
39. Troops

軍馬亦是裸體跣足，右手執摽槍，左手執戰牌，別無所謂弓箭、砲石、甲冑之屬。傳聞與暹人相攻，皆驅百姓使戰，往往亦別無智略謀畫。

白話文**(Vernacular)**：

該國軍隊也是裸體光著腳，右手執標槍，左手執盾牌，別無所謂弓箭、砲石、甲冑之類。傳聞與暹人相攻擊，都驅使百姓作戰，往往亦別無智略謀畫。

The troops are also naked and go barefoot. They hold a lance in their right hand, and a shield in their left hand. They have no bow, arrow, trebuchet, armor, or helmet. It is said that when they fight with the Sien people, they drive ordinary people to fight, usually without a good strategy and plan.

40. 國主出入
40. The Lord In And Out Of the Palace

　　聞在先國主，轍跡未嘗離戶，蓋亦防有不測之變也。新主乃故國主之壻，元以典兵為職。其婦翁殂，女密竊金劍以付其夫，以故親子不得承襲。嘗謀起兵，為新主所覺，斬其趾而安置於幽室。新主身嵌聖鐵，縱使刀箭之屬，著體不能為害，因恃此遂敢出戶。

　　白話文(Vernacular)：

　　聽說以前的國主，從未曾離開其王宮，因為要預防有不測之變。新主乃故國主之女婿，原先是軍人。其岳丈去世，其妻密竊金劍交付給其夫，以致於王子不得承襲王位。王子曾陰謀起兵，為新主所發覺，斬其趾而安置於密室。新主身穿聖鐵盔甲，縱使刀箭之類，不能危害他的身體，因恃此遂敢走出戶外。

　　I heard that the last Lord did not go out of the palace for preventing unforeseen incidents. The new Lord is a son-in-law of the last Lord, and previously he was in charge of the troops. When his father-in-law died, his wife secretly stole the gold sword and gave it to her husband. Consequently, the son couldn't succeed to the throne after his father. He tried to launch a coup, but the new Lord discovered it and chopped off his toes, and imprisoned him in a secluded room. The new Lord wears sacred iron armor, which can prevent knives and arrows from harming him. Relying on that, he dares to go out of the palace.

余宿留歲餘，見其出者四五。凡出時諸軍馬擁其前，旗幟鼓樂踵其後。宮女三五百，花布花髻，手執巨燭，自成一隊，雖白日亦點燭。又有宮女皆執內中金銀器皿及文飾之具，制度迴別，不知其何所用。又有宮女，手執摽槍、摽牌為內兵，又成一隊。又有羊車、鹿車、馬車，皆以金為飾。

白話文(Vernacular)：

我在此留宿一年多，見該國主出宮外四、五次。凡外出時，諸軍馬為前導，旗幟鼓樂接在後面。宮女三、五百人，穿著花布，髻上戴花，手執巨燭，自成一隊，雖白日亦點蠟燭。又有宮女皆執宮中金銀器皿及文飾之器具，制度不太一樣，不知其做什麼用？又有宮女手執標槍、標牌為宮內衛兵，又成一隊。又有羊車、鹿車、馬車，都裝飾黃金。

I stayed in this country for more than one year. I have seen the Lord out of the palace four or five times. When he comes out, a lot of soldiers go out in front, and the next flags and drumming bands follow. About three or four hundred palace girls dressed in flower clothes and flowers tied in their hair-knot, carry large candles in their hands and group themselves as a team. Even in the daytime, they light the candles. Other palace girls carry gold and silver wares of the palace and finely decorated instruments which have different styles and qualities; I don't know what the purpose for it is. Again other palace girls carry lances and shields and group themselves as a contingent of the palace guard. There are carts pulled by goats, deer, and horses; all of them are decorated with gold.

　其諸臣僚國戚，皆騎象在前，遠望紅涼傘不計其數。又其次，則國主之妻及妾媵，或轎或車，或馬或象，其銷金涼傘何止百餘。其後則是國主，立於象上，手持金劍，象之牙亦以金套之。打銷金白涼傘凡二十餘柄，其傘柄皆金為之。其四圍擁簇之象甚多，又有軍馬護之。若遊近處，止用金轎子，皆以宮女擡之。大凡出入，必迎小金塔金佛在其前，觀者皆當跪地頂禮，名為三罷。不然，則為貌事者所擒，不虛釋也。

白話文(**Vernacular**)：

　該國諸大臣、官員和國戚，皆騎象走在前面，遠望去紅涼傘不計其數。又其次，是國主之妻、妾及婢女，或乘轎或車，或馬或象，其鑲金涼傘何止百餘頂。在其後面則是國主，站在象上，手持金劍，象之牙亦以金套之。打鑲金白涼傘凡二十餘頂，其傘柄皆是黃金打造。其四圍擁簇之象甚多，又有軍馬保護。國主若到附近地區，是乘金轎子，都是由宮女擡之。大體上，國主出入，必迎小金塔金佛為其前導，參觀者皆應當跪地頂禮，名為三罷。不然，則為官員所逮捕，短期內不會釋放。

All the ministers, officials, and the Lord's relatives are riding on the elephants in front. Seen from far away, there are countless red umbrellas. Next is the Lord's wife and concubines and their servants; some of them take palanquins or carts, some take horses or elephants, and there are over a hundred golden lace umbrellas. After that is the Lord, who stands on the back of an elephant, a gold sword in his hand; the ivory tusks of his elephant also are encased by a gold cover. There are over twenty gold lace white umbrellas, the handles of which are made of gold. Many elephants gather around him, and the troops guard him as well. If the Lord wants to go to a place nearby, he only takes a gold palanquin carried by palace girls. Generally, when he goes out or into the palace, he must worship a small gold stupa and gold Buddha in front of it. Onlookers all have to kneel down on the ground and worship; it is called "San-ba". Otherwise, those disrespectful people should be arrested by the officials, and would not be released in a short time.

每日國主兩次坐衙，治事亦無定文。凡諸臣與百姓之欲見國主者，皆列坐地上以俟。少頃，聞內中隱隱有樂聲，在外方吹螺以迎之。聞止用金車子，來處稍遠。須臾，見二宮女纖手捲簾，而國主已仗劍立於金窗之中矣。臣僚以下，皆合掌叩頭。螺聲絕，方許擡頭。國主隨亦就坐。聞坐處有獅子皮一領，乃傳國之寶。言事既畢，國主尋即轉身，二宮女復垂其簾，諸人各起身。以此觀之，則雖蠻貊之邦，未嘗不知有君也。

白話文(Vernacular)：

每日國主兩次上朝聽政，治事亦無成文規定的程序。凡諸臣與百姓之欲見國主者，皆列坐地上等候國主到臨。過一會兒，聽到宮內隱隱有樂聲，在外方吹螺歡迎。聽說國主住的地方距離辦公處所稍遠，故他乘金車子。片刻間，看見二宮女用纖手捲開簾子，而國主已持劍站在金窗之中了。臣僚以下，皆合掌叩頭。螺聲停止，才允許擡頭。國主隨後就坐。聽說他的坐處有獅子皮一領，乃傳國之寶。政事談完後，國主隨即轉身走進金車子，二宮女再將簾子放下，諸人起身。從此觀察，該國雖是蠻夷之邦，仍知有國君也。

The Lord goes to his office to deal with governmental affairs twice a day; they have no written documents in the official process. Generally, if any ministers or ordinary people want to meet the Lord, they must sit in a row on the floor to wait. After a little while, they hear the faint sound of music from the inner palace, and then outside a conch shell blows to welcome him. I heard that the inner palace is quite a far distance from the Lord's office, so he takes a golden cart. After a while, two palace girls roll up the curtain by hand. The Lord steps out of the cart and goes into the golden window with a sword. All the officials clasp their palms together in greeting and bow their heads. When the sound of the conch shell has stopped, they can raise their head. Then the Lord sits down. I heard that on the seat of the Lord, there is a lion skin, which is an inherited treasure of the country. When he has finished the official affairs and he turns away leaves immediately. The two palace girls lower the curtain again, and everyone stands up. From this we can understand, although this is a barbarian state, everyone knows that they have a monarch.

國家圖書館出版品預行編目資料

真臘風土記中英文對照本 = Record on the custom and land of Zhen-la(Chinese v. English version) / 周達觀作；陳鴻瑜譯. -- 初版. -- 臺北市：蘭臺出版社, 2023.07
　　面；　　公分. --（東南亞史研究；7）
中英對照
ISBN 978-626-96643-7-5(平裝)

1.CST: 文化史 2.CST: 生活史 3.CST: 柬埔寨

738.421　　　　　　　　　　　　　　112007560

東南亞史研究7

真臘風土記中英文對照本

著　　者：周達觀
譯　　者：陳鴻瑜
總　　編：張加君
編　　輯：陳鴻瑜
美　　編：陳鴻瑜
封面設計：陳勁宏
出　　版：蘭臺出版社
地　　址：臺北市中正區重慶南路1段121號8樓之14
電　　話：(02) 2331-1675 或 (02) 2331-1691
傳　　真：(02) 2382-6225
E - MAIL：books5w@gmail.com或books5w@yahoo.com.tw
網路書店：http://5w.com.tw/
　　　　　https://www.pcstore.com.tw/yesbooks/
　　　　　https://shopee.tw/books5w
　　　　　博客來網路書店、博客思網路書店
　　　　　三民書局、金石堂書店
經　　銷：聯合發行股份有限公司
電　　話：(02) 2917-8022　　傳真：(02) 2915-7212
劃撥戶名：蘭臺出版社　　　帳號：18995335
香港代理：香港聯合零售有限公司
電　　話：(852) 2150-2100　傳真：(852) 2356-0735
出版日期：2023年7月 初版
定　　價：新臺幣450元整（平裝）
ISBN：978-626-96643-7-5